DEATH AS A SALESMAN

DEATH AS A SALESMAN

WHAT'S WRONG WITH ASSISTED SUICIDE

SECOND REVISED EDITION

BRIAN P. JOHNSTON

NRP

New Regency Publishing
Sacramento, California
www.nrpub.com

Death As A Salesman. Second Revised Edition

Cover Design - Robert Aulicino, Pro-Art Design
Photos: Kevorkian, page 47, and his paintings, page 50: *Frontline*, PBS Medicine, page 27: CMCD, Inc.

Although the author and publisher have exhaustively researched all sources and made every effort to ensure the accuracy and completeness of information contained in this book, we assume no responsibilities for errors, inaccuracies, omissions, or any inconsistency herein. Any slights of people, places, or organizations are unintentional. *Readers should immediately consult professionals and seek intervention when dealing with the suicidally depressed or individuals with psychological disorders.*

Library of Congress Cataloging in Publication Data
Johnston, Brian, 1955-
  Death as a salesman : what's wrong with assisted suicide / 2nd revised/ Brian Johnston,
-- Sacramento, CA : New Regency Pub., 1998.
  p. cm.
Includes bibliographical references and index.
ISBN 0-9641125-1-5 : $14.95
1. Assisted suicide--Moral and ethical aspects. I. Title.
R726.J64 1998
174'.24--DC20   98-32841
                                                     CIP 4/98

ACKNOWLEDGEMENTS

Many individuals have contributed to both the content and the tenor of this book, and it would be impossible to name them all. Three, David O'Steen, PhD.; Darla St. Martin; and Burke Balch, J.D.; were significant in their critical contributions. D.B. Warner, Roxanne Trujillo, Richard White, Mike Spence, and Doug Dwyer were helpful and patient proofreaders. Innumerable others offered passing observations, tattered clippings, and helpful insights, their goal – to help ensure that the susceptible are protected at their moment of greatest danger, when they are without hope and at risk of their very lives. It is my hope that this book contributes to that goal of protecting the vulnerable.

Dedicated to my father,

John B. Johnston,

He accomplished many things in his life, yet for him it was important to remember the sick and bring comfort to the afflicted.

PREFACE

There are books already available regarding assisted suicide. Unfortunately, many of them romanticize the practice. A few do bring assisted suicide into question, and these are, by and large, very good books.

This book's purpose is to provide straightforward answers to the question, "What's wrong with assisted suicide?" I can assure you that there are many, many answers to that simple question. Unfortunately, those answers are often offered in medical, legal, or technical terms.

It is my hope that the answers in this book are not complicated or technical. (They are provided for those - and there are apparently a few of you - who are not yet bioethicists.) What I have done here is attempt to examine this issue and the emotional issues surrounding it, in a way that the average person would. You see, it is regular people who are being talked into ending their lives. It is normal people who are being asked to discard nearly three thousand years of medical and social ethics; to change the laws that currently protect the ill, the infirm, the depressed, and the disabled. And it is everyday, sensible people who will make a difference in stopping a very aggressive euthanasia movement. They are the ones who, when confronted with decisions, need practical answers to deal with the traumas of life and death.

In these pages you are going to meet Derek Humphry and Jack Kevorkian, two of the better known and more effective salesmen of the assisted suicide movement. We will look at how they use the media, and how at times the approach taken by the media itself has done more to promote assisted suicide than even its advocates.

Sadly, we will see how this sensational approach to reporting about suicide has in fact led to more and more suicides and requests for suicide. This power of suggestion is demonstrated in the suicide clusters that appear wherever a group of people, large or small, accepts suicide as a possible answer to the challenges of the moment.

We will look at the seamier side of what is happening in the

Netherlands, and at an official Dutch government report on euthanasia in that country. For history buffs there are separate chapters on medical and social ethics, and for you debaters, a special question and answer section with references back to the text. The pages with gray borders indicate particularly useful information for protecting the vulnerable. I have given special attention to dealing with fear and pain, two of the most emotional and needlessly effective weapons in the euthanist armory.

I hope you find this book useful. In contemplating assisted suicide, society is considering a dramatic departure from the values that teach us to respect and protect the vulnerable and the innocent. But remember that society isn't government officials; society is really just normal people like you and me. As you evaluate assisted suicide, consider carefully, for lives are at stake. Ultimately, the life you save may even be your own.

Brian P. Johnston

"The man who kills a man kills a man. The man who kills himself kills all men. As far as he is concerned, he wipes out the world."
- G.K. Chesterton

"To run away from trouble is a form of cowardice, and when it is true that the suicide braves death, he does it not for some noble object, but to escape some ill." - Aristotle

"The man who, in a fit of melancholy, kills himself today would have wanted to live had he a week." - Voltaire

"Guns aren't lawful
Nooses give
Gas smells awful
You might as well live."
- Dorothy Parker, "Resume"

"If you do not know how to die, don't worry. Nature herself will teach you in the proper time; she will discharge that work for you; don't trouble yourself." - Michel de Montaigne

"Do not seek death. Death will find you. But seek the road which makes death a fulfillment." - Dag Hammarskjold

"Be sure to send a lazy man for the angel of death."
- Jewish proverb

"Honor a physician with the honor due unto him." - Ecclesiasticus

"I prefer old age to the alternative." - Maurice Chevalier

"Old age. It's the only disease, Mr. Thompson, you don't look forward to being cured of." - Herman J. Mankiewicz and Orson Welles, CITIZEN KANE

"Hold back those who are being drawn toward death."
Book of Proverbs

CONTENTS

Chapter One

Derek Humphry, Death Salesman

- The Hemlock Society is the world's largest, most effective euthanasia advocacy group.

- Hemlock owes its foundation and growth to one man, Derek Humphry.

- Humphry rose to notoriety after the "assisted suicide" of his first wife, Jean, and the publication of his book, *Jean's Way*.

- Through Humphry's efforts, the work and message of Hemlock eclipsed the other members of the International Right to Die movement.

- The circumstances surrounding the suicide of Humphry's second wife, Hemlock co-founder Ann Wickett, cast a shadow over the apparent motives of assisted suicide advocates.

Derek Humphry, death salesman

Derek Humphry is a man who, on first meeting, can best be described as "intriguing." He speaks in a deep and sonorous British accent. His words are weighted and firm. Though not overbearing, he definitely carries a commanding presence. And his message is clearly one of conviction, for this is one man who has practiced what he's preached.

Humphry's background — advocacy journalist

Humphry was a principal co-founder of the Hemlock Society, the most active and influential euthanasia advocacy group in the United States, if not the world. He is a prolific writer who spent eleven years with the *Sunday Times* of London, as well as writing for the *Daily Mail*. Humphry is proud of his work as an advocacy journalist, having focused on "cutting- edge" issues like "race relations, policing and civil liberties."[1]

But his best-known writings were not to appear in newsprint, though they did employ his creative advocacy skills. His book, *Jean's Way*, is the story of how he facilitated the suicide of his wife Jean, and was written in conjunction with his new wife, a young American woman named Ann Wickett.

Humphry was living in England at the time of the death and he was the only witness to the suicide. We readers are left with few options other than to accept his version of events. (Years later his co-author Ann would cast new light on the death of Jean Humphry, and Derek Humphry's methods of "comforting" his ailing wife would take on a new dimension.)[2]

In *Jean's Way*, Humphry, with Ann's aid, movingly tells the story of Jean Humphry's bout with cancer. The vulnerable Jean, according to a pre-arranged agreement, asked Derek "Darling...is this the day?" As he put it, "It was the most awful moment of my life. However, I had to answer, 'Yes, my darling, it is.'" He then prepared a lethal concoction and served it to her. Humphry admits,

First wife's "assisted suicide"

> ...I asked myself if I should cross-examine her about the correctness of her part of the decision. However, I resisted this because *it was so apparent that she was dependent on me for judgement.* To raise any doubts at this point would only muddle the certainty and clarity of our instincts and intelligence. We both knew intuitively that this was the right time. To waver would have been wrong. (*Jean's Way*, p.185 [emphasis this author]

Two things are immediately apparent from Humphry's telling of the story. Derek himself was to decide when Jean would die. It was his decision, not hers. Secondly, according to this description, Jean exhibited a classic psychological condition displayed by the gravely ill: the desire for affirmation, the self-deprecating "cry for help." Her needs were clearly of an emotional nature.

Typical to assisted suicide — it is usually the "assistant" who makes the ultimate decisions

The book and tabloid coverage of the "assisted suicide" brought him notoriety in Great Britian which lead to Humphry's questioning by the authorities. In time however, all charges were dropped due to the lack of conclusive evidence. But Humphry had found a new cause to advocate, a cause in which he was now not merely a "reporter" but an active participant.

As the dust-jacket reads on a reprint edition, the suicide and the book about it, "launched him on a campaigning career for the right to lawful physician aid in dying."[3]

The founding of Hemlock[4]

In 1978 with his new wife and co-author Ann, Humphry moved to the United States. He picked up a writing job with the *Los Angeles Times*. In 1980, from their base in California, the Humphrys founded the Hemlock Society, and began an assertive takeover of the international Right to Die movement.

There was some division in the right to die movement at that time. Many in the existing "right to die" societies were accepting of what they termed "passive euthanasia" which at times could simply involve the cessation of extraordinary treatment. In these cases that a patient died a natural death from the underlying illness.

Allowing to die is qualitatively different from causing to die

But "passive euthanasia" is a dangerously indefinite term; it could also involve the removal of basic and minimal comfort care, like food and water for quadriplegic patients. In such cases the patient does not die from any underlying illness, and this certainly could not be described as a "natural death." They were simply disabled people who literally died of thirst. Nevertheless, the "passive" euthanists drew a bright line of distinction between themselves and "active" euthanists.

As "active euthanasia" was rejected by some in the right-to-die movement as dangerous and aggressively utilitarian, in the early

1980's many self-described, "passive euthanists" opposed Humphry's radical notion of another individual taking lethal measures against a patient, even if it was with the victim's consent. The conflict between the two groups grew to the point that Humphry's advocacy books were banned by some who only approved of "letting people die."

Hemlock opposed by "passive euthansists"

"Timid" euthanists defeated

In 1984 Humphry succeeded in his second attempt to win election as vice-president of the International Societies for the Right to Die. Having been rebuffed by them once before, Humphry acted quickly to deal with the passive euthanists in the brave new battle for euthanasia. After his election he proclaimed that, "We have moved into a new societal phase." In the October 1984 edition of the *Hemlock Quarterly* Humphry wrote,

> At the 1978, '80, and '82 conferences, the "passive" euthanists held sway... at the '82 Melbourne conference I was refused permission to sell *Let Me Die Before I Wake!* [his active-euthanasia "cookbook" guide to lethal formulas and their administration.] Passive euthanasia... was always an unrealistic argument, a soft, halfway house of the timid... Now we have to wake up politicians and lawyers to the fact that society is asking them to rewrite the laws on dying, suicide, assisted suicide, so that the medical profession is clear about what society wants of it.[5]

Hemlock's growth

From that point on the Hemlock Society's influence grew rapidly. A member of the media himself, Humphry was quite at home in using the tools of the trade. According to Ann, his speaking skills seemed to improve the more he put himself in the public eye. He recognized that he had the ability to mesmerize an audience, and he enjoyed it.

As an experienced agent of the media he knew how to use it with effect. And he did. Hemlock began to gather a lot of support among other "media types" as well. Betty Rollin, who had been a broadcast journalist for NBC and ABC, was involved with the death of her mother, and wrote of it in her book *Last Wish*. She became a vocal supporter of Hemlock.

Humphry and Rollin worked the media circuit

In 1991, publisher Steven Schragis, a

The author, left, interviews Humphry, 1987

Hemlock member, published *Final Exit,* yet another death "how-to" book by Humphry. Because of his commitment Schragis personally oversaw its marketing until it became a number one best-seller.[6]

Religious support

While advancing "doctor-assisted suicide," one of the standard arguments offered by Humphry and other Hemlock advocates was that their single greatest opponent was the Catholic Church. It was strongly implied that this was inappropriate in "our pluralistic society." Invoking the tried and true "separation of church and state," the Catholic Church's concern for public policy was dismissed as medieval, or worse. Yet ironically, one of the greatest single organizing tools at the disposal of Hemlock Society was the Unitarian Church. Much of Hemlock's growth was due to the active involvement and support of the Unitarian-Universalist community.

Catholic Church vilified

During its formative years, Hemlock local organizational meetings in California were regularly held in Unitarian churches.[7] Their 1985 National conference was held at the San Francisco Unitarian Church and conference center. The headquarters for Oregon's Proposition 16 (which was to become the nation's first law legsalizing assisted suicide) were in an office complex adjoined to Unitarian Church headquarters in Portland.[8] It would not be unfair to characterize Unitarian Church support as pivotal in Hemlock's public-policy efforts.

Unitarian Church — backbone of grass roots support

Strong support is also found amongst other "religious" societies. According to Humphry, the Congregational Church is an official supporter.[9] The American Humanist Association, which could certainly be said to be a group with a decidedly religious predilection also embraces "limited" euthanasia. (The 1994 Humanist Hero Award was given to Jack Kevorkian.)

It is clear that "organized religion" has been as much involved in supporting assisted suicide as in opposing it. But it is only the beliefs of opponents that have been criticized in the press; the religious inclination of supporters has received little criticism or analysis.[10]

Tough questions

Although Derek Humphry was frequently before the public eye, he himself rarely got careful scrutiny. Perhaps it was because of his facility with the media, or because they didn't ask the right questions. Nevertheless, there were some questionable aspects to Derek Humphry's approach to the difficulties of life. With just a little probing it was clear that Humphry advocated that euthanasia should eventually be employed for those who were not dying, in addition to the terminally ill. Alzheimer's patients, and the non-terminal handicapped should also be "granted the right" under his world view.[11]

But Humphry's real scrutiny was to come when his second wife was diagnosed with cancer.

Ann's way

Ann Wickett had been a silent partner with Derek, editing his writing and developing publicity. But she was also a partner with him in another endeavor. She facilitated, with him, the double suicide of her parents, an act she later regretted.[12]

Ann had misgivings about a lot of things. She had been a co-founder of Hemlock, she had even coined the name. But now she was having second thoughts. Her real "wake-up call" came when she was diagnosed with breast cancer; instead of receiving his support and sympathy she felt coldly rejected by her husband. It was exactly the opposite of what she had expected. She originally had thought that Derek had truly acted out of love when he "helped" Jean die. Now she wondered.

Second wife alleged she was manipulated toward suicide

Ann admitted publicly that the famous question, "Is this the day?" was asked only once and that they didn't discuss and discuss it, as Derek had insisted. She thought when she wrote the book that Jean had really wanted to kill herself, so Ann felt it was necessary to depict Jean as the decision maker. But when Ann was stricken with cancer herself and was rejected by Humphry, she thought back to Jean's suicide.

> Now, though, after what I've been through, I see her so differently. And I will always find myself wondering what Jean would say if she could speak. I suspect it would be rather chilling.[13]

She admitted that she had helped Derek

by "sanitizing" the story of his relationship with his first wife, omitting from the book the fights and arguments, and most ominously, omitting the fact that the lethal "concoction" had failed to do its work on Jean. Ann said that Humphry had in fact suffocated her.[14]

First wife's death "sanitized"

She was tired of being surrounded with death. She feared Derek. With the inheritance from her parent's death Ann and Derek had bought a farm outside Eugene, Oregon. But once she had been diagnosed, Derek apparently found lodging elsewhere. The real blow came when she was summoned to a Hemlock board meeting and told that she was removed. The rejection she felt was unbearable. Her good friend, Julie Hovarth, took up her cause and called the press about her outlandish treatment.

The *New York Times* ran the story, "Right to Die Group Shaken as Leader Leaves Ill Wife." Ann was asked to appear on *Larry King Live*. Derek called just before the show and left a message on her answering machine. Slowly and deliberately he said,

> If you continue this stupid fighting one step more, I shall give your sister and nieces a full statement that you committed a crime in helping your parents to die. They will then be able to sue you for the return of the three hundred thousand dollars you inherited. Just live quietly, regain your health, agree to a divorce where we keep our own property, and let's get on with our lives. Otherwise, I fly to Boston. I'm deadly earnest. Think it over.[15]

She went ahead with Larry King's program. She later told the *American Medical*

News that she had misgivings about the right-to-die movement, and that not enough emphasis was given to providing a supportive environment to those with life-threatening illnesses. This she knew well, for her own illness and depression left her feeling very alone.

On October 8, 1991, like so many others who have absorbed the literature of death, Ann killed herself. But not without first letting the world know that Derek had "done everything conceivable to precipitate my death."[16]

Wickett commits suicide

Derek Humphry continues his advocacy of assisted-suicide and euthanasia. He has left the Hemlock Society, re-married (to a presumably brave woman), and started a new organization, the Euthanasia Research and Guidance Organization, or ERGO. His deep resonant voice still fills meeting halls and radio waves, and he continues to be an effective ad-

Advocate for Suicide Group Found Dead

EUGENE, Ore., Oct. 9 (AP) — The woman who co-founded the Hemlock Society, an organization that advocates a right to assist in the suicide of the terminally ill, was found dead on Tuesday, and her former husband said he believed that she ha~

wilderness area, where she had parked her pickup and horse trailer.

The authorities declined to speculate on a cause of death. Although an autopsy was performed on Mrs. ~ ~ings were

The Humphrys, who together founded the Hemlock Society, went through a difficult divorce last year, and Mrs. Humphry had been afflicted with breast Mr. Humph~ nar

Ann Wickett committed suicide in October of 1991.
NEW YORK TIMES, *October 10, 1991*

vocate for his cause. However, there remains a shadow over his work, and without doubt, it is the shadow of death.

NOTES

1 Humphry himself frequently invokes these credentials when being interviewed by impressionable journalists. See backflap of *Final Exit.*

2 Humphry's questionable handling of his wives' illnesses is widely documented.

3 Derek Humphry and Ann Wickett, *Jean's Way* (Dell 1991).

4 While this chapter focuses on the Hemlock Society and its co-founders, it does not mean to ignore the existence of other euthanasia advocacy organizations. Hemlock is arguably the most assertive in its conscious attempt to manipulate the media. **Choice in Dying** in New York City is the major distributor of advance directives and is the oldest group in the "death with dignity movement." It was formed in 1991 from the merger of the **Society for the Right to Die** (which until 1975 had been called the Euthanasia Society of America) and **Concern for Dying** (which in 1978 sprang from the remains of Euthanasia Educational Council).

There are other organizations that want to do more than just talk, but actually facilitate individual acts of euthanasia. **Compassion in Dying** was organized in Washington state by the Washington state Hemlock chapter. According to Ralph Mero, their executive director, their goal is to "assist terminally ill patients ... and their families. The group has physicians and other trained persons willing to be present at the time of death." Compasion in Dying challenged the assisted suicide laws of the state of Washington, which resulted in the *Glucksburg* case. The United States Supreme Court overturned the sweeping appealate ruling in this case; it expressly authorized nonvoluntary euthanasia for the incompetent.

The **Death with Dignity Education Center** of San Mateo, California has announced intentions of opening a death center as soon as the law allows.

5 *Hemlock Quarterly*, October 1984.

6 *New York Times*, August 26, 1991. D1

7 Attended by the author.

8 Author attended the meetings in California, interviewed Proposition 16 leaders in Portland offices.

In 1988 the Unitarian-Universalist Assembly issued a statement resolving,

> *That Unitarian Universalists advocate the right to self-determination in dying, and the release from civil or criminal penalties of those who, under proper safeguards, act to honor the right of terminally ill patients to select the time of their own deaths.*

This resolution was not without dissent, D.W. McKinney, address delivered June 22, 1989, Unitarian-Universalist Assembly, New Haven, CN

9 ERGO web page, [http://www.finalexit.org], 11/12/96.

10 Charles J. Sykes, "The Medical Nightmares: German Doctors/American Doctors," *Catholic League Newsletter*, Vol.14.no.8.

11 Interview with author, August 87. Also quoted in *NRL News*, Dec. 18, 1986. This is consistent with the Hemlock embrace of the *Bouvia* case as a seminal right-to-die decision. Elizabeth Bouvia, who was not terminal, but was quadriplegic, was granted the "right" to kill herself by dehydration in a California hospital, this despite the hospital's protests.

While in his book, *Final Exit*, Humphry clearly endorses assisted suicide for quadriplegics who wish it, the ERGO webpage of 1996 reflects a sanitizing of support for "self-determination" of the disabled. One obvious reason for this, is that the advocacy of euthanasia for the handicapped is starkly utilitarian. For many casual supporters of Hemlock, such a blatant dismissal of the disabled may be alarmingly offensive.

However, Court decisions have already indicated that once released, that particular "genie" can not be put back in the bottle. *It would be impossible to grant a constitutional right to someone who was "seriously ill" and at the same time deny it to someone who was not quite sick enough*, the latter would have to "continue suffering without hope of release."

12 Ann Wickett, *Double Exit*. Also cited in Rita Marker's *Deadly Compassion* (New York: Morrow, 1993).

13 Marker, p. 35.

14 Marker, pg. 34-5

15 Quoted in Marker. Taken directly from tape given to Rita Marker by Ann Wickett.

16 From Wickett's suicide note, reprinted in *People Magazine* and elsewhere.

CHAPTER TWO

HOSPICE –
PATIENT AND FAMILY CARE

- Hospice, which seeks to help both the patient and the immediate family, offers a very real alternative to assisted suicide.

- The immediate family are often the most taxed by the debilitating illness of a loved one. Often they are under more emotional pressure than the patient.

- Unlike hospice, assisted suicide requires no care, little time, and little interaction with the patient, it would seem to help the perpetrator more than the recipient.

- A properly run hospice program offers genuine care and intervention to meet the physical and emotional needs of both patient and family.

- The American Hospice Association is strongly opposed to assisted suicide.

Killing ill patients requires the least care

Assisted suicide is presented by advocates as a way of "helping" individuals who are depressed about a terminal condition. But in fact, helping to kill a patient takes the least time and the least care of all possible options. On the contrary, hospice is an example of how society can empathize with and care for these patients.

Hospice is a special *way of caring* for terminally ill patients, their families, and loved ones; it is not a building or a location. Hospice can take place in an acute-care hospital, at a convalescent hospital, or at a facility that is specially established for that purpose. Often hospice is done in an individual's own home.

Hospice is an "enabler" for patients and families

Hospice care enables patients and their families to live as fully as possible during the final stages of life. The emphasis is on living, not on dying. Those who have participated in hospice often cite the deeply satisfying reward that comes from helping those at the end of life's span cope with the closing of their days.

Clinical and non-clinical

Volunteer intensive, hospice treats the patient and family member as one unit, helping to deal with both the clinical and non-clinical questions surrounding the latter part of our lives. It is made up of a team of professionals and volunteers that includes the patient's own physician and provides a broad range of services to the terminally ill and their families. This inclues medical treatment, medications and medical supplies, home health aides, therapy, twenty-four hour care when necessary, and bereavement counseling.

Caring for family as well patient

Often the family is forgotten in the rush to meet the needs of gravely-ill patients. But these are individuals who are dramatically affected by the illness as well; they need emotional support and intervention.

In addition to their own emotional needs, it is the family and friends, more than anyone else, who will influence the mood and mindset of the patient. They may, even unwittingly, reenforce negative thoughts and attitudes. As has been noted elsewhere, the gravely ill are emotionally vulnerable, and depressed family members may unconsciously reinforce, or even suggest 'suicidal' thoughts.[1] Sometimes it is the family members who are in even greater emotional need than the patient.

Psychologist Elizabeth Kubler-Ross points out that often the patient will come to the place of emotionally accepting the natural end of his or her life, but the family hasn't. She says that ironically, "This is also the time during which the family usually needs more help, understanding, and support than the patient himself."[2]

Family members may, even unconciously, reinforce the wrong messages

"Treatment" influenced by family

When looking at cases of assisted suicide, it is not surprising to see the frequency with which "family support of the decision" is used as a primary justification of the act. Often the final decision maker is not even the patient but a family member.[3] Yet the emotional con-

Emotional condition of family and friends often determines treatment

dition of the family is a very poor reason to kill an individual. Proper hospice care recognizes the pressures on family and friends, and seeks to help them cope with this most difficult of circumstances.

A study published by the *Journal of the American Medical Association* found that when administering pain medication to terminal patients,

> Surprisingly the drugs were given nearly as often "for the comfort" of the patient's family as they were given to reduce the suffering of the patient themselves... [Additionally] in four out of every five cases, nurses who had discretion in administering drugs said that they were treating the patients for the comfort of their loved ones.[4]

Family's distress must be addressed

This and other studies appear to indicate that inappropriate actions are often taken because of a family member's perceptions, and not the patient's. It is apparent in many assisted suicide cases that the family and other caregivers are under severe emotional strain, and the option of "assisted suicide" is a ready relief for *their* emotional burden, and not simply the patient's. Failure to address the strain of loved ones often subjects the patient to greater risk of emotional pressure, and inappropriate "surrogate decision-making" by members of their immediate family.

An unprepared family may even be dangerous

Hospice must intervene to help and guide the distraught family for several reasons: as noted, families are often guided by emotions; they often lack medical information; it is hard to separate their personal interests from the patient's (this can include financial as well as emotional interests[5]); family members often see the patient as they were; they fail to appreciate and often underestimate the capabilities of the ill patient.

These common responses by the unprepared family can often make them a risk, and not a benefit to the patient.[6]

Good hospice care

While families can often be the best source of comfort and care, that doesn't mean that that's always the case. There are other professional and volunteer resources available to the critically ill patient. Hospice seeks to employ all of the available resources that can be marshalled for the terminally ill patient and their families.

Contrary to some misconceptions, true hospice means first, last and always, good medical care. Hospice does not mean medical abandonment or medical neglect. In the name of "hospice" there have been reported cases of withdrawal of all medical care, including food and water. But food and water are essential not just for comfort but for sustaining life itself. In such cases the actual "terminal condition" is no longer the underlying illness, it is dehydration. In dehydration cases, the attending medical staff will often sedate the patient into unconciousness for the patient's last days. This is not appropriate. The patient is not dying from his or her illness, but dying through intentional, controlled neglect.[6] Death from dehydration is often a long and drawn-out process, resulting in greater suffering for the family as the patient slowly grows cadaverous be-

"Hospice" does not include medical abandonment

Not dying from illness, but dehydration

fore their eyes. This is not proper hospice care. It is a form of euthanasia.

Hospice is "a way" of handling terminal illness. And just as in any "approach" it can be taken in different ways. The National Hospice Association opposes assisted suicide, and they joined in the court cases against legalizing it when it came before the U.S. Supreme Court [*Glucksburg* and *Quill*]. But certain individual hospice workers and physicians joined the opposing camp. They filed briefs in support of making assisted suicide legal. It is important therefore, if you are seeking hospice support, to recognize what makes a good hospice program, and what is inappropriate.

Looking for a hospice

There are certain essential qualities to be aware of when looking for a good hospice.

* Is there adequate medical staff?
     Hospice is not medical abandonment.

*Is there particular attention paid to treating chronic pain? It is important to know that there is someone who cares about the pain, attempts to control it while enabling the patient to remain lucid; who stays close to the situation to be able to change the medication as needed.

*Is there 24 hour contact service? If there is any hedging on this, beware. Genuine hospice has round-the-clock service built into it . Hospice is *being there.*

* Is the approach interdisciplinary? The "total pain" of the patient must be addressed.

*Does the program address the family's needs? Family members need support and counsel, sometimes even more than the patient. And in the aftermath, bereavement followup is an integral part of any true hospice program.[8.]

The hospice movement has proved that when adequately guided, families are often the best caregivers providing the most enjoyable and fulfilling environment for the terminally-ill patient. But by the same token, studies in hospice settings indicate that without adequate guidelines and intervention, **the emotional toll of debilitating illness can subject friends and family members to tremendous pressure. Where euthanasia is 'acceptable' and when that pressure is distilled to a simple decision between life and death, death can be a very effective salesman.**

Hospice provides real answers — and lessens the temptation of assisted suicide

NOTES

1 Margaret Pabst-Battin, "Manipulated Suicide," *Bioethics Quarterly* 2 (1980), pp. 123, 134.

2 Elisabeth Kubler-Ross, *On Death and Dying.* (New York: Collier Books, 1969), p.113

3 In nearly all the prominent cases we see the family member making

the final decision, e.g. Humphry and Bob Harper of Roseville, California.

4 *New York Times*, February 19, 1992. C12. Interestingly the article continues, "But on this score, doctors who order the drugs differ in their thinking from nurses who actually administer them. In just over half of the cases did doctors order drugs to comfort the family of the dying patient. Yet in more than four out of every five cases, nurses who had discretion in administering drugs said that they were treating the patients for the comfort of their loved ones."

5 This financial implication, which is frequently present, can have long-term effects on survivors. This is true even if a fiscal benefit was not an express motive.
Ironically, Derek Humphry reportedly put the unsavory onus of "legacy hunting" on his estranged wife, Ann, who had helped to kill her parents in a double assisted-suicide. She inherited hundreds of thousands of dollars. In an effort to gain her silence, he threatened to expose her involvement in the deaths.

6 Ezekiel J. Emanuel and Linda L. Emanuel, "Proxy Decision Making for Incompetent Patients: An Ethical and Empirical Analyses," 267 *Journal of the American Medical Association* 2067, 2068 (1992).

7 It is important to note here that observers [Fenigsen, Hendin, et al] point out that this (dehydration) is precisely the method employed by Dutch physicians before they moved on to giving lethal injections. They recognized they were slowly killing the patients through neglect, so to them it seemed much more humane and compassionate to get it over with and kill quickly.

8 Kenneth Wentzel, *To Those Who Need it Most, Hospice Means Hope* (Boston: Charles River Books, 1981), p. 106.

CHAPTER THREE

THE PROBLEM OF PAIN

• The desire for suicide is a strong indication that the physical and emotional suffering of the patient have not been adequately treated.

• Effective pain management is currently available for even the most painful of cancers.

• Many of assisted suicide's most dedicated advocates (including Pieter Admiraal, "father" of Dutch euthanasia) admit that death by suicide is not a proper treatment for pain.

• Many doctors still need adequate training in pain control. If the doctor isn't treating the pain, don't kill the patient – get another doctor.

• Emotional pain often goes unaddressed. This is often a much greater influence on a patient's decisions than physical pain.

"Putting an end to suffering" is one of the most frequent reasons used by assisted suicide advocates for justifying their ultimate goal - the elimination of the patient. But even some of their own experts admit that this is a fallacy.

Pain is treatable

Dr. Pieter Admiraal, recognized as one of the pre-eminent leaders of the Dutch euthanasia movement has said, "There are many good reasons for euthanasia, but pain control is not one of them."[1] The pain of even the most difficult of cancers can be treated and the patient does not have to be "knocked out" or "doped silly," if proper pain management techniques are used.[2]

At present, the medicine, knowledge and technology is available such that adequate pain control measures can be implemented to control the pain of up to 99% of patients.[3]

Untreated pain

Request for suicide indicates poor treatment

It is when pain, both physical and emotional pain, goes untreated, that patients can emotionally react by asking to "get it over with." The request to die therefore, is often a strong indication that there is underlying pain that is not being treated. This pain can be physical, emotional, or psychological.

> We frequently see patients referred to our Pain Clinic who request physician-assisted suicide because of uncontrolled pain. We commonly see such ideation and requests dissolve with adequate control of pain and

other symptoms, using combinations of
pharmacologic, neurosurgical, anesthetic,
or psychological approaches.

Dr. Kathleen Foley
Chief of Pain Services
Memorial Sloan-Kettering
Cancer Center, New York.[4]

Dr. Cicely Saunders, a British physician who
has been at the forefront of the modern hospice movement has put it this way:

When someone asks for euthanasia or
turns to suicide, I believe in almost every
case someone, or society as a whole, has
failed that person. To suggest that such an
act should be legalized is to offer a negative and dangerous answer to problems
which should be solved by better means.[5]

Physician training

One of the problems patients have in receiving good pain management is that very
often their physicians are not adequately
trained to deal with it. Often physicians are
using outmoded or inadequate resources to
diagnose and treat pain. Until recently, few
medical schools have required specific courses
in pain management techniques prior to
graduation.[6]

Pain management training has not been required of physicians

The inadequacies of doctors' training in
this area was partially addressed on March 2,
1994, when the federal Agency for Health Care
Policy and Research issued new guidelines for
health professionals outlining systematic assessment for pain and proper medication or
treatment to relieve it.

The Federal guidelines were designed to help physicians overcome their hesitations regarding certain drugs so they can adequately control cancer pain. "Doctors have the tools and the capability to do that effectively and to assess the pain regularly and systematically," says Patricia Greene of the American Cancer Society.[7]

Medication myths

Proper pain management is not followed because of ignorance

Another of the problems in the dispensing of pain control is the overcoming of misconceptions. "There are a number of myths keeping patients from taking (pain) medication," says Greene, who is National Vice-President for Patient Services at the American Cancer Society in Atlanta. "They're afraid it won't make a difference, worried about side effects, and concerned about addiction. But these concerns are unfounded. With the proper use of analgesics and opiates you can keep 'terminal' patients comfortable for a very long time."[8]

The lack of training and widespread misconceptions allow unnecessary fears to restrict the type of treatment offered. One of the most common errors which hampers effective pain management stems from the fear of dealing with a controlled substance.

Fear of addiction

While frowned on by some physicians untrained in pain control, opiates like morphine and other narcotic drugs are useful when used in a graduated (or *titrated*) treatment, and in combinations with other forms of pain management. "They are a relatively safe drug to use," says Dr. Stuart Grossman of the John Hopkins Oncology Center in Baltimore. "The goal is to keep patients comfortable,

Narcotic drugs are only one form of pain medicine. They are primarily useful when used in a graduated (or *titrated*) treatment, and in combinations with other forms of pain management.

and you can do that for many months with opiates."[9]

Many well-meaning doctors will provide inadequate pain management out of fear of creating a "worse evil," addiction, in their patient. But the threat of addiction in these cases is usually without foundation.

Addiction is not a real threat

> There is tremendous confusion about addiction and substance abuse in this country – confusing people involved in street crimes with the legitimate use of morphine and other opiates for pain relief. We have reviewed the scientific evidence exhaustively. There is little or no evidence to support the fact that people who take these drugs for pain relief become addicted.
>
> Dr. Richard Payne
> MD Anderson Cancer Center
> Houston, Texas[10]

Fear of admitting pain

Patients themselves can also pose barriers to their own pain treatment. A reluctance to report pain for cultural or psychological reasons can leave a patient's true needs unmet.

Dr. Robert Miller, a medical oncologist and medical director of Sutter Hospice Program in Sacramento, says that

> Many people believe that reporting a symptom of pain is a sign of weakness. They're reluctant to do that in front of the doctor or in front of the family. They also feel that by recognizing they have pain, it means their cancer is getting worse.[17]

Dr. Richard Pratt, co-author of *You Don't Have to Suffer*, notes that pain is sometimes difficult to assess because patients won't admit to it. "You can't see pain in a blood test or an X-ray, assessing it requires a good relationship between doctor and patient."[18]

These psychological games wreak havoc on a physician's ability to diagnose and treat pain. And while the pain goes untreated, it is not uncommon for patients to want to escape their world of suffering.

Fear of pain's "image"

Many associate malignant illness with physical pain; many associate dying with physical pain. But surprisingly this is often not the case at all! It is often the *idea* of impending physical pain and suffering that individuals will react to with fear. It is this fear which needs to be overcome.[11]

Amazingly, according to some of the world's experts on pain management, many of those who die a natural death do so without any actual physical suffering. Matthew Conolly, M.D., of UCLA Medical Center, cites studies that indicate that "at least a third of all patients dying of malignant disease suffer no pain at any time."[12] (But, as noted elsewhere, there may well be a period of *emotional pain* and sorrow during the dying process. This stage may not require medication, but often requires encouragement and counseling.[13])

Hospice physician Stuart Shipko states that

> In my work with terminally ill patients I have never seen a patient who needed to be "put to sleep" to ease his or her suffering. It is a common fear that death is preceded by tremendous pain or a gasping for air, but in reality pain and oxygen hunger are more a part of chronic syndromes than of terminal ones.[14]

Relatively few terminal patients suffer from chronic pain

Family's fears

On many occasions it is not even the fear held by the patient that causes inappropriate action. Often the fears and insecurities of those closest to the patient, the family and close friends, have a dramatic influence on the treatment given. A study published by the *Journal of the American Medical Association* in February 1992 found that pain-killing drugs are administered as often "for the comfort" of the patient's family as they were given to soothe

the suffering of the patients themselves.[15]

Very often family members themselves need intervention in order to help them deal with the emotional stresses and psychological pain of a loved one's illness. Without adequate intervention, those closest to an ill individual may inadvertently reinforce detrimental psychological messages.[16]

Dealing with "total pain"

Emotional anguish *must* be treated

Often patients who have a severe, debilitating, or terminal illness suffer emotional pain in addition to their physical pain. This suffering can be based in a fear of social rejection or inferiority, or mental anguish over the implications of the illness. These emotional pressures can magnify any physical discomfort present. Effective pain control therefore requires a team effort of doctors, nurses, psychiatrists, counselors, and family members to address *all* the pain the patient is suffering.

Total pain

Dr. Cicely Saunders, herself an expert on pain management and a guiding light in the establishment of the hospice movement, characterized this sum total of a patient's wrestling with malignancy as "total pain." It is the job of the care-givers to treat this total pain, and to realize that it is often composed of mental, social, and spiritual suffering as well as any physical pain.[19]

Avoiding a "final solution:"
Ed Hoch's story

At 71, retired salesman Edwin Hoch had bone cancer (one of the most painful of cancers) and was literally racked with pain. He was bedridden and nearly immobile. He fit the classic profile of the assisted suicide "candidate," being much worse off than, say, Patricia Cashman of San Marcos, California, Kevorkian's 26th victim. (She had bone cancer which had gone into remission before she made her appointment with Kevorkian.[20]) But Ed Hoch without question had a terminal condition and was literally paralyzed with pain. "I almost stopped all of my activities except for breathing and eating," he told *USA Today.*[21]

Then in January of 1994 he received a combination treatment of radiation and morphine to treat the cancer and its accompanying pain. By February, Hoch had returned to his hobbies which include repairing and maintaining his collection of antique clocks and watches, a pastime which requires great patience and fine motor skills.[22]

Combination treatment for pain

Ed Hoch's story is one of thousands which take place everyday. Proper pain mangement allows patients with chronic pain or terminal diagnoses to pursue interests and relationships that are so important during critical illnesses. Failure to recognize and treat the "total pain" of a patient can often lead to fear, aprehension, and depression.

> If you or a loved one is suffering from intolerable pain and your physician is not dealing with that pain, the answer is simple - and it is not the killing of the patient. The real answer is much more incisive, and much more caring - get another doctor.

Notes

1. Dr. Pieter Admiraal, speech before the Biennial Conference of the Right to Die Societies, Maastricht, Holland, 1990. Dr. Admiraal is an anesthesiologist. He therefore, perhaps better than his fellow euthanasia advocates, knows that medicine has a tremendous and effective array of pain-management medicines available. He writes:

In fact, for most patients "cancer pain" means real physical pain combined with fear, sorrow, depression, and exhaustion. This kind of "pain" is an alarm signal indicating shortcomings in interhuman contact and misunderstandings of the patient's situation. One can treat this "pain" with good terminal care based on warm human contact. *(Free Inquiry* 9 [1989], No. 1.)

Admiraal does not endorse euthanasia for "pain" but for a "diminished quality of life."

2. A. Jacox et al, *Management of Cancer Pain, Adult's Quick Reference Guide*, No. 9. U.S. Public Health Service, 1994.

3. Judy Kornell, *Pain Management and Care of the Terminal Patient* (Washington: Washington State Medical Association, 1992), p. 4.

4. Kathleen M. Foley, "The Relationship of Pain and Symptom Management to Patient Requests for Physician-Assisted Suicide," *Journal of Pain and Symptom Management* 6 (July 1991) 290, quoted by Burke Balch and David Waters in "Why We Shouldn't Legalize Assisted Suicide", *Bul-*

letin of the Medical Ethics Department, National Right to Life Committee, May 1994.

5. Cicely Saunders, "Caring to the End," *Nursing Mirror* 4, 1980.

6. In 1987 the Medical Board of the State of California issued new regulations requiring all medical students to take a course in pain management prior to graduation. California physicians had no such requirement before that time.

7. "Controlling Pain as Part of Cancer Care," *USA Today*, March 2, 1994, D7.

8. Ibid.

9. Ibid.

10. Ibid.

11. Franklin Roosevelt, who himself had faced debilitating illness, movingly addressed this truth. He offered words of encouragement during World War II that are useful in our everyday lives; but particularly when we have to face the unknown: "The only thing we have to fear," he said, "is fear itself."

12. Twycross and Lack, *Therapeutics in Terminal Care* 9 (1984), quoted by Dr. Matthew Conolly, Associate Professor, Medicine and Pharmacology, University of California, Los Angeles, in "Alternative to Euthanasia: Pain Management," *Issues in Law and Medicine* 4 (1987) No. 4.

13. Elisabeth Kubler-Ross, *On Death and Dying* (New York: Collier, 1969).

14. Stuart Shipko, M.D., *Los Angeles Herald Examiner*, Letters to the Editor, October 4, 1987.

15. *Journal of the American Medical Association*, February 19, 1992, quoted by the *New York Times*, February 19, 1992, C12. The study, as reported in the *Times*, goes into even greater detail:

> Doctors who order drugs differ in their thinking from nurses who actually administer them. In just over half the cases did doctors order drugs to comfort the family of the dying patient. Yet in more than four out of every five cases, nurses who had discretion in administering drugs said that they were treating the patients for the benefit of their loved ones.

16. Ibid. As noted above, it is documented that the loved ones them-selves may incite inappropriate treatments. And as noted elsewhere in this book, it is often the family, those who are in "the first line of de-fense" against depression, who, overwhelmed or depressed themselves, may often send *precisely the wrong signals* to a suicidal individual.

17. Robert Miller, M.D., in interview with author.

18. *USA Today.*

19. Cicely Saunders, *The Management of Terminal Malignant Disease* 232 (1984), quoted by Dr. Matthew Conolly, Associate Professor, Medi-cine and Pharmacology, University of California, Los Angeles, in "Alter-native to Euthanasia: Pain Management," *Issues in Law and Medicine* 4 (1987) No. 4.

20. *Contra Costa Times*, Nov. 18, 1995, B1.

21. *USA Today.*

22. Ibid.

PROTECTING
THE VULNERABLE
SOME GUIDELINES
TO MANAGEMENT OF CANCER PAIN

Flexibility is the key to managing cancer pain. As patients vary in diagnosis, stage of disease, responses to pain and interventions, and personal preferences, so must pain management.

HIGHLIGHTS
OF PATIENT MANAGEMENT

Effective pain management is best achieved by a team approach involving patients, their families, and health care providers. The physician should:

- Discuss pain and its management with patients and their families.

- Encourage patients to be active participants in their care.

- Reassure patients who are reluctant to report pain that there are many safe and effective ways to relieve pain.

- Consider the cost of proposed drugs and technologies.

- Share documented pain assessment and management with other clinicians treating the patient.

DEALING WITH PAIN

- Know state/local regulations for controlled substances.

RECOMMENDED CLINICAL APPROACH

- **Ask** about pain regularly. **Assess** pain systematically.

- **Believe** the patient and family in their reports of pain and what relieves it.

- **Choose** pain control options appropriate for the patient, family, and setting.

- **Deliver** interventions in a timely, logical, coordinated fashion.

- **Empower** patients and their families. **Enable patients to control their course to the greatest extent possible.**

BARRIERS TO CANCER PAIN MANAGEMENT

Problems related to health care professionals:

- Inadequate knowledge of pain management

- Poor assessment of pain

- Concern about regulation of controlled substances

What's Wrong with Assisted Suicide

- Fear of patient addiction
- Concern about side effects of analgesics
- Concern about patients becoming tolerant to analgesics

Problems related to patients

- Reluctance to report pain
- Concern about distracting physicians from treatment of underlying disease
- Fear that pain means disease is worse
- Concern about not being a "good" patient
- Reluctance to take pain medications
- Fear of addiction or of being thought of as an addict
- Worries about unmanageable side effects
- Concern about becoming tolerant to pain medications

Problems related to the health care system

- Low priority given to cancer pain treatment
- Inadequate reimbursement:

    The most appropriate treatment may not be reimbursed or may be too costly for patients and families

- Restrictive regulation of controlled substances

• Problems of availability of treatment or access to it

PAIN ASSESSMENT

Failure to assess pain is a critical factor leading to undertreatment. Assessment involves both the physician and the patient. It should occur:

• At regular intervals after initiation of treatment

• At each new report of pain

• At a suitable interval after drug therapy

Follow-up assessment

Continual assessment of cancer pain is crucial. Changes in pain pattern of the development of the new pain should trigger diagnostic evaluation and modification of the treatment plan. Persistent pain indicates the need to consider other methods and alternative treatments.

Drug therapy is the cornerstone of cancer pain management. It is effective, relatively low risk, inexpensive, and usually works quickly.

Physical, emotional, and social interventions

Patients should be encouraged to remain active and participate in self-care when possible. Non-invasive physical and social activities can be used along with drugs and other treatments to manage pain during all phases of care. The effectiveness of these methods depends upon the patient's participation and communication of which methods best alleviate pain.

Treating cancer pain in the elderly

Like other adults, elderly patients require comprehensive assessment and aggressive management of cancer pain. However, older patients are at risk for undertreatment of pain because of underestimation of their sensitivity to pain, the expectation that they tolerate pain well, and misconceptions about their ability to benefit from the use of opioids.

Relaxation exercises

- Slow rhythmic breathing for relaxation

- Simple touch, massage, or warmth for relaxation

- Recalling peaceful past experiences

- Active listening to recorded music

(From MANAGEMENT OF CANCER PAIN, ADULT'S QUICK REFERENCE GUIDE *by A. Jacox et al, published by the U.S. Public Health Service.)*

DEALING WITH FEAR

PATIENT FEAR
AND ANXIETY

One of the most common motives for seeking assisted suicide is an individual's fear and anxiety about the unknown. Dealing with cancer can create the greatest of anxieties.

FEAR OF PAIN: The *fear* of cancer pain can at times be more taxing than the pain itself; this must be fought with a good pain control program and reassurance. Combatting the fear of cancer pain demands:

• Permission to admit the fear, and not be brushed aside

• An open discussion of thoughts and feelings

• Patient participation in the pain relief program

• A calm and positive attitude

• Recognizing that crying is not wrong, either by the patient or the family. (This does not mean hand-wringing or constant hysteria. There is an appropriate time for tears between loved ones as they face the worst crisis of their lives.)

LOSS OF ROLE IN THE FAMILY: This loss can cause the strongest of patients to despair and is a painful time for the family. Communication is important to keep the patient from feeling as if they had already left the world of the living. It is essential for the patient, at all stages of the illness, to hear repeatedly that they are loved. Many times a patient is not asking for answers, but only for someone to listen. When a genuine answer is desired, do the best you can to give an answer. *Never lie or hedge.*

Whenever possible the patient's opinion and advice should be sought; his or her role in the family should be maintained as long as possible. Even though a patient may know he is dying, he can still care about the household, and his normal responsibilities. These things can be discussed without adding to an ill person's worries. Keep the patient involved. ***The small things in life often make its sweetest memories.***

LOSS OF JOB: An individual's job or profession is a very important part of life. It gives many people a sense of being a part of the ongoing world; a world that will soon live on without them. To give up one's job and its prestige is often painful beyond words.

LOSS OF SOCIAL POSITION: For someone who has enjoyed a position of recognition, personal or professional, this social loss can be profound.

SENSE OF HELPLESSNESS: This can be the ultimate loss. Being dependent on other people for every want and need is a dreadful experience for many ill people. Extraordinary tact and discretion are required by the family to help the patient adjust to this circumstance. Ill patients are aware of their helplessness; preserve their dignity, let them keep their self-respect. There is a person inside that body. Listen to what that person says; feel that inner sorrow. Drugs can carry the body's pain, only another can lift the soul's.

DISFIGUREMENT: Many illnesses, even the most subtle cancers, regardless of the site of the cancer, take an incredible toll on the entire body. Patients know that the shocking changes in appearance may be upsetting to the family. Do not abandon them; do not isolate them. They know that some friends and relatives will avoid looking directly at them during conversations. When they feel this discomfort in family and friends their misery intensifies, their days become bleak, long, and dark.

FEAR OF NURSING HOME: Many cancer patients have a fear of being placed in a nursing home. They know that their care is an extra burden on the family. This fear of institutional care is very real. Depending on the circumstances, such institutional care is often not necessary. Visiting-nurse care, home hospice, or a few months of family self-sacrifice can often be a much more emotionally and spiritually gratifying experience. If a nursing home is chosen, utmost care should be taken, and frequent visits and involvement are necessary.

LOSS OF BODY CONTROL: *This demoralizes the patient more than any other aspect of the illness.* This requires discretion and tenderness by the family, but they should never show pity. Pity is the last thing the patient wants, and at times is almost more than they can bear.

FAMILY FINANCES: A real cause of anxiety when illness strikes the head of the household, it can be an enormous worry if he or she is the sole breadwinner.

WORRY ABOUT SPOUSE AND CHILDREN: Anxiety causes a spouse to be desperately terrified for the future of his or her mate. Even if there are adult children, will they care for the remaining parent? If the patient has small children, what will happen to them?

FRIENDS DO NOT VISIT: At the onset of an illness friends and co-workers often visit. As time passes and the illness worsens, some friends become too busy to visit. For a while some will send excuses, but some do not even bother to do that. Many people cannot bring themselves to be in the presence of death and the dying. They tell themselves, "I want to remember him as he was." The ill person learns who the real friends were. *This is a time of dread and loneliness for the patient and the family.*

SPIRITUAL AND EMOTIONAL LOSS: As many hospice volunteers know, the fears and sorrow of the impending end of life can cause great emotional discomfort. For some patients it may be the first time they have examined a spiritual reality they had dismissed. Many who seek assisted suicide apparently do so in an attempt to avoid this emotional and spiritual pain. These spiritual issues should be addressed, and not avoided.

(From THE LONELY PAIN OF CANCER: HOMECARE FOR THE TERMINALLY ILL *by Peabody and Mooney, Sharp Publishing. Used by permission.)*

CHAPTER FOUR

DOCTOR DEATH, JACK KEVORKIAN

- Kevorkian implies that he plays a passive role in death; but he is the arbiter of who among his "patients" is to die, and when he or she is to die. He actively facilitates each death.

- A pathologist by training, his practice involved diseased cells and cadavers, not living patients.

- While many of his "patients" had a debilitating illness, few, if any, could have been classified as "dying."

- He has always held a macabre fixation with death: "Maybe it's the boy in me!"

- An artistic dilettante, he paints bizarrely distorted pictures of child cannibalism, detached organs, maggot infested corpses, and severed heads. He has tried, in vain, to promote Hitler's art.

He has his own fan club. He has called himself the intellectual heir of Einstein, Thoreau, and Martin Luther King. And in 1990 Jack Kevorkian told a judge his struggles to promote assisted suicide were comparable to "the birth of Christianity."

In later court cases Kevorkian would insist, for legal reasons, that he was not intending to kill people, "only relieve their pain."

"He's no killer. He doesn't want people to die," according to Geoffery Fieger, his attorney, "Dr. Kevorkian never intended to assist the deceased to commit suicide."[1]

What is he advocating?

In order to understand what Jack Kevorkian does, and what "assisted suicide" really is, it is first important to understand what it really is not. Contrary to what has been asserted by Kevorkian, using carbon monoxide is not a form of pain control, it is not acceptable treatment for pain; administering it can only result in death. He does not merely "observe" these deaths or "attend" them. He orchestrates and facilitates them.

He does not "observe"

Assisted suicide advocates often cloud the issue and characterize the actual killing in soft, misleading terms, or deliberately lie about what is taking place.

But the debate is not about "pain" or letting people die, reducing cumbersome treatments, or "pulling the plug." It is not about "letting nature take its course," or "accepting a natural and dignified death."

There is nothing natural about the act of assisted suicide. What Jack Kevorkian does has nothing to do with accepting the course of events or gently helping relieve pain. As a so-called "treatment," it is not passive or gentle. It is aggressive, it is invasive, it is ruthlessly final.

Not a "natural" death

Myth of passivity

Weasel words

To bolster the myth of passivity, his press releases claim that Kevorkian "witnessed," "was present at," or "attended" the suicide. These words clearly belie his true actions and his undeniably active role in the killing of the individual. Nevertheless, these passive words which imply mere observation of a patient are typically parroted by the popular media to describe Kevorkian's adventures.[2]

During a true natural death, medical professionals as well as others can and often do "attend" to the basic needs of a patient as nature takes its course. Many professionals will tell of the rewarding aspects of this type of hospice work. But, as the verb "attend" implies, their actions are not causal in the death; they are not agents of their patient's demise. They witness the death in the true sense of the word. One can reasonably say that Mother Teresa attends at a deathbed, for the death will come to pass with or without her presence. But Jack Kevorkian does much more than "attend," he insists on being an agent of death. He is hardly

Mother Teresa "attends" at a deathbed

Kevorkian is an active agent of death

its "witness." In fact, it is only because the patient really isn't dying that Kevorkian's involvement is required at all.

A man of peculiar tastes

From his earliest days, Jack Kevorkian's life and macabre interests have had one focus -- death. During the 1950's as a medical student at the University of Michigan, Kevorkian would often make extracurricular visits to terminal patients, not to comfort them, but to watch them die. He would gaze into their eyes, trying to determine the exact moment of death. When asked about the scientific purpose of this exercise he admitted, "There was no practical application. I was curious, that's all."[3] When asked about his general fixation and enthusiasm for death, his response was, "Maybe it's the boy in me."[4]

Kevorkian was trained as a laboratory pathologist. His practice was in cadavers, not in the treatment of living patients.

Years later, in one of his many arcane articles advocating the use of prisoners to study death, Kevorkian invoked the actions of young medical students during the French Revolution. They would grab heads as they fell from the guillotine and shout into the ears, "Do you hear me?" Kevorkian says they got no response, but the revolutionaries' fasci-

As a medical student — obsessed with death

nation with death intrigued him.[5]

In 1958 Kevorkian presented a paper to the American Association for the Advancement of Science detailing his plan for "terminal human experimentation." Condemned criminals could volunteer for experiments that would intentionally kill them. In 1960 he asserted in his pamphlet, "Medical Research and the Death Penalty" that experiments on humans were much more useful than those done on animals, and killing condemned criminals without experimenting on them was a waste.

Advocates human "death experiments"

But in Kevorkian's economy it is not just death-row inmates who would be candidates for human experimentation. In an article published by the German journal *Medicine and Law*, experiments could be performed on anyone whom Kevorkian felt might face "imminent death." This was interestingly defined to include,

> (a) all brain-dead, comatose, mentally incompetent or otherwise completely uncommunicative individuals; (b) all neonates, infants and children less than (__) years old (age must be arbitrarily set by consensus); (c) all living intrauterine and aborted or delivered fetuses.

Kevorkian and Nazi medical "science"

The near-universal condemnation of human experimentation in the aftermath of the Nazi atrocities did not seem to faze Kevorkian. In 1986 he wrote that the results of the freezing experiments, in which prisoners were dropped into icy water to see how long they would survive, "are not absolutely negative." He insisted that "a tiny bit of practical value for mankind did result."[6] A friend of Kevorkian, Dr. Harold Klawans of Chicago, was irritated with him. He did not want Kevorkian projecting acceptance of those atrocities. Klawans convinced Kevorkian to tone down any mention of those experiments in Kevorkian's 1991 book, *Prescription: Medicide.*

Nevertheless, while talking to the *Detroit Free Press* in 1991, Kevorkian again commented on the usefulness of the experiments and dismissed the plight of the Jews as relatively insignificant when compared to that of his ancestors, the Armenians. The Armenian holocaust involved the killing of millions, and was bloodshed of the most violent sort. But apparently, in his mind, since the Jews were killed clinically, they had it much easier. "The Jews were gassed. Armenians were killed in every conceivable way.... So the Holocaust doesn't interest me, see? They've had a lot of publicity, but they didn't suffer as much."[7]

What is apparently lost on Kevorkian is that it was not just the great numbers of those killed in the Nazi Holocaust that makes it subject to condemnation. It is also the clinical nature of the Holocaust itself, and the willing involvement of physicians (which is widely documented) which makes it so chilling, and so relevant to what he so blithely pursues.

This public concern about the use of "physician-as-killer" appears to be lost on Kevorkian. He is seemingly oblivious to the greater implications of his actions and just

Saw scientific value in Nazi doctors' experiments

The clinical nature of the Holocaust — the involvement of physicians

wants to get back to business. He is in no way intimidated by the legal brouhaha he has generated. "I'm not really frightened by what's happened to me; I'm not even intimidated. I'm annoyed."[8]

Promoting Hitler's art?

Macabre artistic tastes

An artistic dilettante, Kevorkian has produced paintings described by observers as strange, dark, foreboding, and, "obsessed with death." Kevorkian admits to mixing cadaver blood

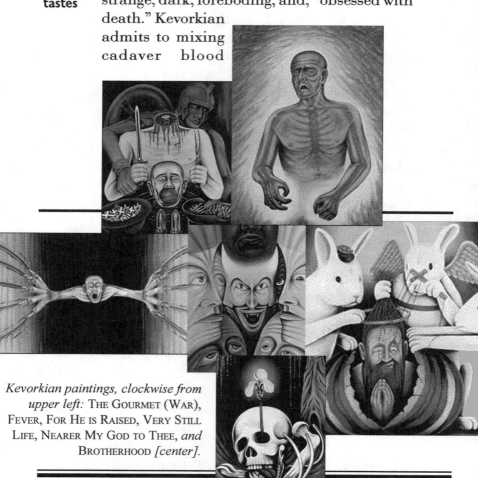

Kevorkian paintings, clockwise from upper left: THE GOURMET (WAR), FEVER, FOR HE IS RAISED, VERY STILL LIFE, NEARER MY GOD TO THEE, *and* BROTHERHOOD [center].

with his own and to using the macabre concoction to paint one of his frames.

But his taste in art really only came to light when it was made known that he tried to promote a tour of Adolph Hitler's artwork. In 1986 Kevorkian contacted Billy Price of Houston to see if Price would allow part of his large collection of Hitler's work to be used for an exhibition. Kevorkian excitedly told Price it would be a "once-in-a-lifetime undertaking." Price declined.[9]

Hitler's art

Years later, when confronted with this, Kevorkian said that he had proposed this as a way to reap something good from the German dictator's wickedness, and that he intended to give some of the money to charity, including a local Holocaust Memorial Center. But this seems oddly contrived given his comments on the Holocaust.

Doctor to the dead

A pathologist by training, just like your county coroner, Kevorkian's expertise was in cadavers and diseased cells. His specialty and day-to-day practice did not involve diagnosing or treating living patients. Only two states had granted Kevorkian license to work as a pathologist, and both of them (Michigan and California) suspended that license. In fact, at the California Medical Board hearing that resulted in his suspension, Kevorkian admitted that he was not qualified to practice medicine, even as a general practitioner.

Not qualified to practice medicine

Professional life

Since his graduation from medical school, Jack Kevorkian led what Michigan investigators called "a checkered career." A rather unremarkable pathologist, he couldn't hold down a job. He bounced from hospital to hospital, and tried to set up his own diagnostic lab in Detroit. After failing that, he went to Hollywood to briefly pursue an unsuccessful film project. He ended his professional career commuting between part-time pathology jobs in Long Beach, sometimes sleeping in his rusty Volkswagen van. In 1985 he returned to Michigan, where he drew Social Secuity benefits and lived off canned food. In 1989 he applied for a job as a paramedic, but was turned down.

New career begins,
launched by Geraldo

After his retirement (what some have called a *forced* retirement), Kevorkian continued to write about and promote his bizarre personal theories and deadly fixation, and tinkered with killing gadgets. In the late 1980's he started to appear as a "serial guest" on afternoon talk shows.

His first official patient to receive "medicide" had seen him on *Geraldo*. Janet Adkins, fifty-one years old, was starting to forget things - like her keys.[9] She had found out from her doctor that she had early-stage Alzheimer's (a slowly-debilitating, degenerative illness that can take from seven to ten years to fully manifest).

But Janet was afraid of what the unknown future might be like. She did not want to go back to her doctor for follow-up. She saw what she wanted on *Geraldo*, called the producer, and got Kevorkian's number. On a balmy summer's day in June of 1990, Janet Adkins was a long way from any form of natural death or serious debilitation. Though depressed about her diagnosis she wanted "to go out in style." She played tennis against her 26-year-old son and won. She was fit and vibrant when she submitted to Jack Kevorkian's treatment. She died instantly.

First victim wanted to die while "healthy"

Such was the case for many of Kevorkian's victims. Of relatively few could it actually be said that death was "imminent." In fact it was precisely because death did *not* seem imminent that they were to be killed.

A natural death was not on the horizon

Thomas Hyde's story

Thomas Hyde was a young man with amyotrophic lateral sclerosis (ALS), or Lou Gehrig's disease. With Kevorkian's help, he went to his death on August 4, 1993. He can be seen, along with Janet Adkins, on videotape broadcast by the PBS program *Frontline*, a taping which was originally arranged by Kevorkian himself.[11] For those familiar with Lou Gehrig's disease, what is striking about young Thomas Hyde is not how ill he was, but in fact how well.

A desperate young man

Observing the broadcast, one notes that while Hyde is clearly debilitated and his speech is slurred, nevertheless he is able to speak. Most

ALS patients lose their powers of speech, but
with assistance go on to face life's challenges.
What is most clear on the tape, is that he is
emotionally distraught over his illness. His vis-
ibly broken wife can no longer handle the emotional strain. She agrees with Thomas, that
taking Kevorkian's route is the best answer.

This may be a touching scene at first
blush. The disease is truly tragic. But Thomas
had many potentially productive, and with the
proper counseling, very happy years before
him.

Those who do not know such individuals
need only think of Stephen Hawking, the bril-
liant physicist who received the Nobel Prize.
He is demonstrably more debilitated and infirm than Thomas Hyde. He cannot speak. He
breathes with a respirator. He cannot walk, but
instead skirts about in his electric wheelchair.
A professor at Cambridge, he has forever
changed the world of physics. And he has accomplished all of this while his illness was
much worse than Thomas'.

With proper medical
care, counseling,
and intervention,
Thomas had the
promise of living

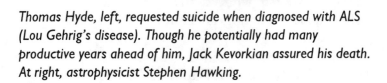

*Thomas Hyde, left, requested suicide when diagnosed with ALS
(Lou Gehrig's disease). Though he potentially had many
productive years ahead of him, Jack Kevorkian assured his death.
At right, astrophysicist Stephen Hawking.*

as an overcomer; but instead he was treated by Jack Kevorkian, a "doctor" who implements only one prescription — medicide.

Youngest victim

On February 26, 1998 Kevorkian killed his youngest victim to date. Roosevelt Dawson, 21, had been paralyzed for one year due to an unusual viral infection that affected his spine. The year of immobility had left Dawson isolated and depressed. During that period he had spoken to Kevorkian several times.

Youngest victim needed to be offered hope

Ironically, the evening of Dawson's untimely demise, a nationwide television broadcast celebrated the achievements of quadriplegics; the need to encourage them, and the need to keep looking for cures. Christopher Reeve and an all-star cast took the opportunity to remind the nation of the value of each individual's life, no matter how incapacitated.

In another ironic twist, the next day, Friday, February 27, 1998, the story of Dawson's death at Kevorkian's hands ran on page three of *USA Today's* weekend edition. The front page of the same paper was emblazoned with a photo of Stephen Hawking. The story described Hawking's visit to the White House, and the inspiring story of his life with disabilities; physical disabilities that more than rivaled Roosevelt Dawson's.

He missed the program

Would young Roosevelt have been inspired by that television show? Would he have been encouraged if he had read that paper? We can never know that. However, we do know this: being encouraged and seeing hope is all that Roosevelt Dawson really did need to live, because he did not die from any illness.

Treating emotional illness with death?

"She could have lived many years if not decades."

Marjorie Wantz, 58, suffered from "psycogenic" pain, sensations perceived by her brain but, according to her doctors and L.G. Dragovic, Oakland County (Michigan) Coroner, lacking a physical cause. But in 1991, she committed suicide "in the presence" of Kevorkian and another victim, Sherry Miller, 43. Miller had been diagnosed by another physician as having multiple sclerosis. But, "she could have lived many years, if not decades," according to Dragovic.[11] Neither of the victims of this double "suicide" would have died a natural death in the forseeable future.

Patricia Cashman of San Marcos, California had had a history of cancer, but it was in remission. A divorcee, she lived alone and kept to herself. Like so many of the other victims, she read Hemlock literature, and was a supporter of Kevorkian's cause.[13]

When she thought the cancer might be returning she went to see Kevorkian. She had often petitioned him for "medicide." On November 8, 1995, she got her request. Parroting Kevorkian's press releases, the newspapers announced that her death was simply "in his presence."

But Patricia had never seen an oncologist (cancer specialist). She did not seek counseling. Her former husband, who saw her occasionally, said, "She had been losing weight, but she never said anything about pain."[14] The coroner could find no cancer. Later, a pathologist hired by Kevorkian's attorney found only microscopic traces of cancer.

But the presence of physical illness was not what Kevorkian was trying to determine; Cashman's state of mind was the issue. It was her request to die that Kevorkian treated, not her illness, whether physical or emotional. He had done no tests. Although her own physician had prescribed a reasonable course of pain medication, she had admitted that she was not taking the prescribed pain pills, "because she wanted to keep a clear head."[15]

Kevorkian does not treat illnesses, he treats emotions.

It is clear that proper counseling and pain management had not been pursued by Cashman. It is just as obvious that neither alternative is a part of the Kevorkian repertoire.

His prescription is death

In Vietnam, a trite maxim was used to justify the burning of villages: "In order to save that village, we had to destroy it." In the same vein, Kevorkian's prescription for a suffering and depressed individual is essentially reduced to the arrogant condescension, "To effectively treat this patient, I had to kill her."

"Every disease that may shorten life, no matter how much, is terminal."[16]
— Jack Kevorkian

He is not alone

While Jack Kevorkian has become the most obvious and notable physician-killer, he is by no means alone in his attempt to dramatically change the nature of the healing arts. Perhaps his one, saving virtue is that he is such an offensively odd character. His compatriots in euthanasia advocacy are often much more pleasant and genteel individuals, and they are typically more artful in their approach.

Dr. Timothy Quill gained notoriety when he published a description of his "assisting" in the death of a young woman. *Death and Dignity; A Case of Individualized Decisionmaking* is a touchingly emotional story of a young woman who was suffering in what was apparently the terminal stages of leukemia. What is unique about the story is that it did not appear in the tony and urbane magazines which often function as advocates of selective euthanasia, but in the very highbrow and usually scholarly, *New England Journal of Medicine*. It was not a study, but an isolated story clearly designed to evoke sympathy from a targeted audience of physicians.

But the emotional situation described by Quill was not without controversy. As with many such narratives, the agent of assisted suicide is free to give his version of events, and there is scant testimony to contest it. Many physicians were alarmed and outraged at Quill's tone, and particularly at his cavalier admission that he refered his patient to the Hemlock society!

Timothy Quill, of *Quill v. Vacco*

Quill, an articulate and well-mannered spokesman, gained further notoriety when he unsuccessfully sought to overturn the assisted-suicide laws of New York state.

Dr. Philip Nitschke is a general practitioner in Australia's Northern Territories. When the provincial government passed a law on September 22, 1996 allowing the practice, Nitschke began supervising the deaths of willing patients. His reasoning was simple, he says he did it because no other territorial doctor was willing.

On March 25, 1997 the national Parliament passed a bill overriding the territory's suicide legislation. But Nitschke continued his grissly practice. "In each case I must decide, 'Can I get away with this or can't I?' If they get help [in suicide], it is because I think I can. If they don't, it is because it is too risky."

One thing about risk - it doesn't bother Jack Kevorkian.

NOTES

1 Geoffrey Fieger, speaking to a Pontiac, Michigan jury; April, 1996.

2 Michael Betzold, author of *Appointment with Dr. Death* (Momentum Books, 1993) has been praised for his even-handed analysis of Kevorkian and his cause. On May 26, 1997, he wrote in the *New Republic*,

> Normally, journalists are cautious in characterizing suspicious deaths and those involved in them. But on the Kevorkian story it is the norm for the press to report as fact whatever [Kevorkian's attorney] Fieger says.... Why are the media so willing to suspend disbelief and accept the view of the man accused of participating in the homicide? The answer, ultimately, is about the biases journalists bring to their jobs.... The man who covers Dr. Death for the *New York Times*, Jack Lassenberry, a Detroit freelancer who is the *Times*'s principal writer on Kevorkian, pretends objectivity in his *Times* pieces. But... (he) betrays his views, describing Fieger as "a brilliant lawyer" who "seems to be on the brink of changing history"; Kevorkian as a compassionate doctor who "has standards"; and the police who pursue

Kevorkian as the "Keystone Cops... ." Lassenberry has written dozens of articles on the Kevorkian beat for the *Times*, and those pieces have changed the tone of the *Times*'s coverage from critical to favorable, portraying Kevorkian in a notably sympathetic light. Lassenberry has also published pieces flattering to Kevorkian and Fieger in *Esquire*, *George*, *Vanity Fair* and other publications."

3 Mark Hosenball, "The Real Jack Kevorkian," *Newsweek*, Dec. 6, 1993, p.28

4 *Time*, May 9, 1994, p.18

5 Hosenball, p.29.

6 Ibid.

7 *Detroit Free Press*, April 1991

8 Speech to the American Humanist Association, Dec. 1994.

9 *Detroit Free Press*, May 18, 1994.

10 *Frontline*, PBS August 1995.

11 Ibid.

12 *Detroit Free Press*, April 19, 1996.

13 *San Diego Union Tribune*. Nov 9, 1995.

14 Ibid.

15 Ibid.

16 Kevorkian speaking to the National Press Club, Washington, DC, October 7, 1992.

CHAPTER FIVE

DUTCH TREAT

- Assisted suicide is widely practiced in the Netherlands under supposedly "limited" circumstances, but these limitations and "safeguards" have proven unworkable.

- Government reports show that thousands of people have been put to death when no request for suicide has been made. In 1990 alone, 5,941 individuals (more than half of those euthanized), were killed without their consent.[1]

- The Dutch experience demonstrates that a society's acceptance of voluntary euthanasia for "hard cases" has rapidly led to the acceptance of involuntary euthanasia (killing an individual when there has been no such request).

- The Dutch government, through the Ministry of Health, continues to sponsor programs to soften resistance to the practice of euthanasia.

- The Dutch Supreme Court has upheld the "assisted

suicide" of the non-terminal, supporting the death of an otherwise healthy, 51 year-old woman who was clinically depressed. The same court has authorized lethal injections for handicapped infants.

• Many Dutch citizens are afraid to see a physician if they are suffering a serious illness.

Today, on *A Matter of Life and Death*, our guests are two cancer patients both in need of the same expensive new drug... a drug that could possibly save their lives. But only one will be eligible. You, our studio audience, will be given the opportunity to consider the facts of these cases and vote on which patient you think should receive the treatment! And now the host of our show... Heeeeeeere's Violet!

Although the above scenario may sound surreal, like a scene from the theater of the absurd, it is unfortunately all too real. It is a rough translation of the content of an actual Dutch TV program.

A Matter of Life and Death is a popular television series hosted by Violet Falkenberg, and co-sponsored by the Dutch Ministry of Health.

Dutch government seeks to imbue citizens with a sense of cost-cutting duty

In the program the audience members are actually asked to choose life for one contestant over another. The contestants are real patients facing serious medical decisions. Although the audience does not in reality have the authority to make the final decision as to who gets the treatment, they respond enthusiastically to the chance to exercise their judgment and theoretical "power of execution."

Medical rationing is prevalent in the Netherlands and the purpose of the show, according to a spokeswoman for the Dutch Ministry of Health, is to instill in the mind of the public the fact that not all illnesses and conditions can be given the same consideration; that due to enormous health care costs, choices must be made.

Although euthanasia is still officially "prohibited" by Dutch legal statute, due to several sweeping rulings by the Dutch high court it is nevertheless a protected activity, widely practiced and rarely prosecuted. It is an action allowed under the legal concept of *force majeure* and regulated by guidelines accepted by the Secretary of Health, the Health Council, the Board of the Royal Dutch Society of Medicine, and the judiciary. **Euthanasia still officially prohibited**

Originally, *force majeure* was an acknowledgement that the doctor has the right to overrule the law if he deems it is in his patient's best interests. *Force majeure* was applied to justify extreme actions taken when necessary to *defend* life. Ironically, its meaning has been inverted and it is today employed as the legal underpinning which justifies the taking of life.

Public opinion

In light of the concerted effort to change public opinion, it should come as no surprise to find that acceptance of voluntary euthana- **Public opinion** sia is increasing. Two Dutch polls suggest 70% of the people accepted active euthanasia in 1985; 76% in 1986. It is popularly portrayed by the media as an act of human freedom.

However, an analysis of public opinion also shows that the "freedom" is not meant for everyone and popular opinion holds that society has a right to cut short a person's life when it is deemed unworthy. "Life-saving treatment should be denied the severely handicapped, the elderly and perhaps, to persons without families.... A majority of the same public that proclaims support for ...freedom of choice and the right to die, also accepts involuntary active euthanasia–that is, denial of free choice and of the right to live," says Dutch doctor Richard Fenigsen.

A majority also support involuntary euthanasia

Although polls consistently show the Dutch favor the use of euthanasia, opinion is generally determined by circumstances. One poll of the elderly found that while half of those living independently favored euthanasia, almost all of those in nursing homes opposed it. More than half of those living in an institution said that they personally feared being killed without their permission.[2] Violet Falkenburg and the Dutch Ministry of Health seem to be doing their job.

Majority of the dependent fear involuntary euthanasia

Duty to die

The Dutch public has been dramatically influenced by the idea that euthanasia is the right to self-determination and freedom of choice. It is a commonly held view that this is a person's duty and responsibility to himself, to society and to his family. However, this is where a subtle but powerful shift in emphasis changes the character of assisted suicide; if it indeed is considered a *social duty*, then it immediately loses the quality of being *voluntary*.

Not voluntary if a *duty*

In spite of widespread public acceptance of these ideas, there also exists a strong undercurrent of suspicion, distrust, and fear of the medical community. Resentment toward doctors' ability to keep people alive has fostered the right to die movement, but ironically, many are now terrified of hospital or convalescent treatment. They realize that under the new ethical system they have little control over their own lives once they are placed under a physician's care.

Fear of medical community

Development of the euthanasia philosophy

How did this come to pass? Dutch physician and euthanasia opponent Richard Fenigsen tells us in "A Case Against Euthanasia." He points out that early twentieth century German philosophers developed the concept of "balanced suicide." According to this theory, an individual could rationally evaluate his life situation, find it unacceptable, and foreseeing no significant change in the future, decide to end his life. German thinkers such as Haeckel, Jost, Binding, and Hoche introduced the concept of lives "unworthy of life," and advocated the extermination of these useless individuals.

> Appearing on the scene half a century after their German predecessors, after the experience of Nazi euthanasia on psychiatric patients and the handicapped, after

Europe's historical experience of genocide, and at a much further advanced stage in the development of... human rights, the champions of euthanasia in The Netherlands had to present a modified and highly refined program. They emphasized the right to die, and stressed death as a relief from suffering and as being in the best interest of those who were ill and unhappy– a program designed to appeal to those who believe in human rights. This program, promoted by talented writers... kept gaining support until an avalanche effect occurred. Editors and publishers soon became reluctant to print or broadcast anything that went against the current. The media have been virtually monopolized by the euthanasia proponents, and a whole generation of Dutch people has been raised without ever hearing any serious opposition to it."[3]

The nation noted for its brave resistance of Nazi euthanasia, for its Corrie ten Booms, for its Anne Franks; has now adopted the very ethic they so valiantly resisted a few short decades earlier.

A best-seller

"Meaningless lives"

In 1969, Dutch physician Dr. Jan Hendrik Van den Berg wrote a highly influential book, *Medical Power and Medical Ethics*, which states that unconditional respect for human life is an ethic of the past. His vivid pictures of human suffering and serene depiction of euthanasia strongly influenced Dutch opinion. He argued that, for their own sake, defective children must not be allowed to live; and that doctors have a duty to terminate "meaningless" lives. He condemns families who do not request euthanasia and asserts that neither the patient's nor the family's consent is necessary to carry it out. In case of a family's refusal, a committee of doctors and laymen should impose the decision. The book was a huge success and is now in its twenty-fifth printing.[4]

Ideas do have consequences. From the philosophers, to the "experts" in the fields of medicine, psychiatry, and law; from authors and journalists to the electronic media with its game shows attempting to heighten public consciousness - Dutch culture has been influenced by a concerted attack on the long-held idea that human life has sanctity.

The Assen case

In Assen, Holland, in the spring of 1993, Dr. Boudewijn Chabot was acquitted for assisting in the suicide of one of his patients. The fifty year-old woman, given the fictitious name of "Netty Boomsma," was physically healthy but depressed over the loss of her sons and a divorce from her husband.

According to the ruling, Chabot, a psychiatrist, was justified because he met the criterion for *force majeure*: he considered it necessary to put his patient's "welfare" ahead of the law; he felt the patient was competent to make the decision; and he considered her suffering to be *irremediable*. He had not even gotten a second opinion.

The nation's largest daily, *De Telegraaf*,

Psychiatrists authorize death for the depressed

declared that the government had crossed, "a bridge too far;" but mental health organizations welcomed the ruling. Marianne van den Ende, a spokesman for a mental health group, said the decision "allows the emancipation of the psychiatric patient."[5]

Mental suffering sufficient

This decision now extended the Dutch practice of assisted suicide and euthanasia to the treatment of suicidal patients who are not physically ill. Chabot believed his patient was not clinically depressed and had no psychiatric illness, but was simply suffering and wanted to die.

The Assen case points to the precipitous downhill momentum - from assisted suicide to euthanasia; from euthanasia for the terminally ill to those who are chronically ill; from physical suffering to mental suffering; from requiring a patient's request to administering lethal doses solely at a doctor's discretion.

Accepting a depressed suicidal patient as eligible for assisted suicide endangers other depressed patients, particularly those who may not respond quickly to treatment. The legalization of a final solution to their temporary problems is a callous and ominous departure from what has been society's historical efforts to protect their lives and restore their fragile emotions.

Government study

In order to shed more light on what was

really happening within its own borders, the
Dutch government comissioned the Attorney
General of the Supreme Court, Professor J.
Remmelink to undertake a major study of how
assisted suicide and euthanasia were actually
being practiced, given the absence of prosecution. The Committee to Investigate the Medical Practice Concerning Euthanasia, released
its conlusions, dubbed the "Remmelink Report" at the end of 1991.

Dutch government report revealed abuses

The Remmelink Report is of great value
in that it contained the most extensive and
reliable information on euthanasia in the
Netherlands gathered to that date (Sept. 10,
1991).

Dr. Richard Fenigsen relates much of the
detailed findings from this report in his article, "The Report of the Dutch Governmental
Committee on Euthanasia." printed in *Issues
in Law and Medicine*, Volume 7, Number 3,
1991. The findings reveal that annually 25,306
cases of euthanasia occurred in the Netherlands. This included 2,300 cases of active voluntary euthanasia, 400 cases of physician assisted suicide, and 1,000 cases of active involuntary euthanasia. In 5,800 cases, life-prolong-
ing treatment was withdrawn upon the
patient's request and 82% of those died. In
8,750 cases, life prolonging treatment was withdrawn *without* the request of the patient and
was done with the intent to terminate life.
22,500 patients died of overdoses of morphine.
8,100 of these (36%) were done with the intent
to terminate life. The 25,306 cases of euthanasia constitute 19.4% of the 130,000 deaths
that occur in the Netherlands each year.

Official Dutch report

Fenigsen notes that, to the total number

of euthanasia cases, unspecified numbers must be assumed to include the termination of newborns with disabilities, children with life-threatening diseases, psychiatric patients, and patients with AIDS, as according to the report, termination of life is practiced in these cases as well.

Involuntary euthanasia

The figures published in the Remmelink Report indicate that 14,691 cases, or 11.3% of the total number of deaths in the country, were by involuntary euthanasia. But the committee concluded that only 1000 cases were "a deliberate action to terminate life without the patient's consent." The remaining 13,691 cases of involuntary euthanasia are listed in the report under different names. For instance, the 4,941 cases where a *lethal overdose* of morphine was administered without the patient's knowledge are listed under the subsection, "Pain Relief."

Other important findings include:

• In 8% of the cases, physicians proceeded to active involuntary euthanasia even though they believed that other courses of action were still possible. "Low quality of life," "no prospect of improvement," and "the family can't take it anymore" were among the most frequently cited reasons to terminate a patient's life without the knowledge of the families.

Death certificates falsified

• The "rules of conduct" were often disregarded. Many general practitioners disregarded the rule to consult another physician; over half omitted recording the proceedings in writing; 72% of the doctors concealed voluntary euthanasia in the death certificates; and in cases of involuntary euthanasia, the doctors, with a single exception, never stated the truth in the death certificates.

This report caused the Dutch government to acknowledge that the practice of both voluntary and involuntary euthanasia were taking place and to save face, propose some regulations subjecting it to their control. The following regulations were proposed in 1993:

1) Euthanasia and assisted suicide continue to be legally prohibited and punishable crimes.

2) Doctors who carry out active euthanasia upon request, or actively terminate a patient's life without his or her request should report the case to the coroner who will inform the district attorney. (This was voted as an amendment to the Coroner's Act.)

3) No judicial inquiry should be started by the district attorney if the circumstances of the case indicate that the doctor acted with due conscientiousness and care. It is assumed the **Non-** doctor acted carefully if he followed the rules **binding** of careful conduct.[6] **regulations**

These regulations were not binding. There were no punishments stipulated for violations. They merely acknowledged officially what had been in practice for two decades, and they "encouraged" reporting. The reporting form now includes reporting on both euthanasia upon request, and *without the patient's request.*

Direct killing of patients in the Netherlands in 1990*				
	Active Euthanasia	Physician-assisted suicide	Morphine overdose intended to terminate life	Total
With patient's consent	2300	400	3159	5859
Without patient's consent	1000		4941	5941
Total	3300	400	8100	11,800

Figures used in this table are drawn from the source noted below: Medische Beslissingen Roknd Het Levenseinde: Rapport van de Commissie Onderzoek Medische Praktijk Inzake Euthanasia (Medical Decisions About the End of Life: Report of the Committee to Investigate the Medical Practice Concerning Euthanasia). The Hague (1991), ISBN 90 39 90124 4 (2 volumes).

There is no punishment for failure to report.

In 1995 a follow-up study found that 83% of acts of physician-implemented euthanasia are unreported.

The first Rule of Careful Conduct, that the patient must express a voluntary and emphatic wish for euthanasia, has essentially been made void by the regulations, which (since the form asks that it be reported) in principle now permit **involuntary** euthanasia. Through equating *voluntary* and *involuntary* euthanasia, the "regulations" have now put the medically dependent, or anyone unable to express their will, in a particularly vulnerable position.

Involuntary euthanasia authorized

Dutch euthanasia's movers and shakers

Dr. Herbert Cohen is probably the best known physician in the Netherlands whoing consults on euthanasia cases. Cohen and most physicians prefer physician-determined euthanasia to assisted suicide. You must remember that assisted suicide implies that the "patient" is the decisionmaker. Cohen reasons that there are often problems when the patient themselves try to take action. There is always a chance that patients will vomit medication taken orally; or the dosage may be insufficient; or because medicines react differently from patient to patient, there may be complicated reaction.

The doctor should decide

Though some physicians might just "leave the pills" for a suicidal patient, for Cohen it is preferable to directly and personally have a hand in the death. It's much more efficient. "The first time you do it, euthanasia is difficult... You think it would be easier to write a prescription... (but) you are responsible for the effect when it's taken. You have to be... ready to terminate the life if something goes wrong. I do it [write lethal prescriptions] only if a patient strongly demands it."[7]

Cohen, like many other physicians, is against the 1994 legislation requesting doctors to report all cases of involuntary euthanasia. As long as these practices are still "illegal," it seems silly to him to expect someone to turn himself in for a crime. He believes that death is influenced by a doctor's decision in almost all non-traumatic cases and that death should be a doctor-orchestrated event.[8]

Rene Diekstra, who co-authored a book on suicide and assisted suicide, was instrumental in helping to foster current Dutch opinion on the subject. He even devised the guidelines for the rules of conduct. In contrast to Cohen, he believes that assisted suicide is a better way than euthanasia to ensure that each act is voluntary. His own observations and experiences have revealed the difficulty involved in reaching that goal. He is disappointed that euthanasia well-exceeds assisted suicide in use, and he is certain that because of the use of involuntary euthanasia, many people are being killed who do not have to die.

Even assisted suicide advocates are troubled by widespread abuse

Herbert Hendin, American suicidologist who moved to the Netherlands to observe the Dutch experiment, tells us,

> Diekstra was troubled that his vision of providing relief from suffering when no other relief was possible in a way that preserved patient autonomy was lost in the realities of euthanasia in the Netherlands. He was disturbed that a system he helped to father wrongly put to death more people than the relatively small number who met Dutch criteria for appropriate euthanasia or assisted suicide.[9]

Children killed

Professor P. Voute, the country's leading specialist in pediatric oncology, revealed that he has given some of the children under his care a poison that enables them to commit suicide when they feel so inclined. He says that he averages six cases a year, sometimes with the consent of the parents and sometimes without their knowledge.[10]

In 1993, Dr. Henk Prins gave a handicapped newborn infant a lethal injection. On Wednesday, April 26, 1995, the Dutch Supreme Court ruled that the doctor, in killing the child, was guilty of murder. The murder, however, was justifiable in light of the liberal "rules of conduct" governing euthanasia. In handing down the ruling the presiding judge wished him "all the best in the future."[11]

Prins felt it was a positive step forward for doctors; Dr. Fenigsen considers it a step closer to mass extermination for children with disabilities.

Nun's involuntary death

In another notorious case, a Dutch doctor gave a lethal injection to a Catholic nun who was suffering during her terminal illness. He assumed she did not ask for euthanasia because her religion prevented her and so he made the decision for her.[12]

The inevitable appeal to cost

Cost-cutting is frequently involved in justifying euthanasia, says Dr. Fenigsen:

> Doctors allow at least 300 handicapped newborn Dutch babies to die every year; prevent surgery for congenital heart disease in Down's syndrome children by refusing to give anesthesia; and refuse to implant pacemakers for heart block in patients older than seventy-five or to treat acute pulmonary edema in the elderly and in single people without close family. Some doctors justify these practices by arguing that it is in those patients' own best interest to die as soon as possible, but often the explanation is that society should not be burdened with keeping such persons alive. The decisions are taken without the knowledge of the patients and against their will.[13]

In such cases doctors clearly violate the code of medical conduct. However these practices are still widely supported by members of the public, theologians, and the medical authorities.

Prosecutions

The law   According to Fenigsen, the majority of the legal profession also support assisted suicide and euthanasia. Judges, prosecutors, and lawyers regularly prefer to protect doctors who practice questionable cases of euthanasia, instead of seeking protective rulings for their "patients."

The current guidelines are so vague that even when they are not followed, if brought to trial, judges have almost always ruled in favor of the physician on the grounds of *force majeure*.

Mass killings

Clearing out senior homes   In 1985, reports emerged on a suspicion of twenty killings in the De Terp Senior Citizens' Home in The Hague. The doctor in charge

> pleaded guilty to five, was accused of four, and convicted of three killings. Witnesses testified that some of the victims were not ill but only senile and querulous and that the doctor was impatient with elderly people, reluctant to treat them, frequently absent, and he left many decisions to the male nurse. The latter carried out the killings (using untraceable intravenous injections of insulin) and threatened other De Terp inhabitants with euthanasia.... The Board of the Royal Dutch Society of Medicine was alarmed, not by the killings but by the conviction of the doctor, which could cause feelings of insecurity among

physicians who help their patients to die and could discourage these doctors from doing so openly. A higher court dismissed the accused doctor's guilty plea and found him innocent of the killings, while a civil court awarded him 300,000 guilders ($150,000) in damages.[14]

In the Assen case mentioned earlier, Dr. Chabot did go to trial, and was defended by Eugene Sutorius, the most prominent attorney in the Netherlands defending physicians in euthanasia cases. Chabot's actions in "Netty Boomsma's" suicide were clearly inappropriate. Considering her condition "incurable" was questionable and so was assuming that a patient's refusal of therapy is justification to help her die. Hendin tells us,

> Time alone could have altered her mood. None of Chabot's consultants had actually seen Netty, and they were not unanimous in their support. Experts like Schudel, who had written an opinion disapproving of the action, were not called. The only expert witnesses called were for the defense. The only expert witness recommended by the prosecutor wrote an opinion justifying Chabot's actions.[15]

Mild prosecution

Herman Feber, a prosecutor specializing in euthanasia cases, said he felt the lawyer chosen to prosecute this case was reluctant to take it. Feber knew the prosecutor and his sympathies and felt that he had been ordered by the Ministry of Justice to try this case for political reasons.

Feber also mentions that if a doctor wants, he can easily assist suicide secretly. Only if he reports the case without fulfilling the conditions can he be prosecuted. But in the Assen case, Dr. Chabot had followed the rules of careful conduct, had not provided other treatment for Netty, and had not had other consultants see the case on the grounds that it would be too distressing for the patient to see another doctor.

> The Dutch Supreme Court which ruled on the Assen case in June 1994 agreed with the lower courts in affirming that mental suffering can be grounds for assisted suicide but found Chabot guilty of not having had a psychiatric consultant see the patient. Although the court expressed the belief that such consultation was particularly necessary in the absence of physical illness, it imposed no punishment, since it felt that in all other regards Chabot had behaved responsibly.[16]

Dutch experiment's clearest message: "limited euthanasia" is not controllable

Professor Joost Schudel, chairman of the department of psychology at Erasmus University, has a firm answer to the question of who decides whether a patient who cannot speak for himself lives or dies: the doctor decides. He believes the opinions or desires of relatives should not influence the doctor's decision. Hendin comments that the relationship between doctor and patient has reached a new, and dangerous dimension - the wishes of the doctor are ascribed to be those of the patient.[17]

Full-circle

Dutch right-to-die advocates sought to free themselves from what they considered to be a "controlling" medical profession. Ironically they have created a culture that has given them despotic and absolute control to physicians –

whether they like it or not.

The Dutch experiment with assisted suicide has demonstrated that "safeguarding euthanasia" is unworkable. The acceptance of voluntary euthanasia for "hard cases" has rapidly led to the acceptance of involuntary euthanasia; the Dutch government itself has admitted that thousands of patients have been put to death when no request for suicide has been made.

AUSTRALIA

While the world's focus has been on euthanasia as it is practiced in the Netherlands, it is important to note that it still is not actually legalized in that country.

In July of 1996 the legislature of the Northern Territory authorized assisted suicide for the terminally ill. However, after further consideration (and four deaths), the National Parliament voted overwhelmingly to overturn the law on March 25, 1997.[18]

COLOMBIA

On May 27, 1997, Columbia's highest court legalized euthanasia for those who had, "clearly given their consent." The Constitutional Court ruled that, "a judge will have to determine the circumstances for each case." The actual practice of Columbian euthanasia is yet to be adequately documented.

NOTES

1 *Medische Beslissingen Roknd Het Levenseinde: Rapport van de Commisse Onderzoek Medische Praktijk Inzake Euthanasie* (*Medical Decisions About the End of Life: Report of the Committee to Investigate the Medical Practice Concerning Euthanasia*). The Hague (1991) ISBN 90-39 90124 4 (2 volumes)

2 Michael Fumento, "What the Dutch Can Teach Us About Euthana-

sia," *The Washington Times*, March 19, 1995, B3.

3 Richard Fenigsen, "Euthanasia in the Netherlands," 6 *Issues in Law and Medicine* 3 (1990), p. 234.

4 Ibid., p. 229.

5 Associated Press, "Dutch Court Expands Euthanasia Guidelines to Include Mentally Ill," *Los Angeles Times*, June 23, 1994, home edition, A18.

6 Hebert Hendin, "Seduced by Death: Doctors, Patients, and the Dutch Cure," 10 *Issues in Law and Medicine* (1994) 2, pp. 129-130.

7 Fenigsen, Report of the Dutch Government Committee on Euthanasia, *Issues in Law and Medicine* 7 (1991) 3.

8 Hendin, p. 138.

9 Ibid., p. 142.

10 Reuters News Service, "Dutch Court Expands Law, Upholds Euthanasia of Baby," *Los Angeles Times*, 27 April 1995, home edition, p. A4.

11 Fenigsen, "Euthanasia in the Netherlands," p. 242.

12 Fenigsen, "A Case Against Dutch Euthanasia," *Hastings Center Report*, Special Supplement, January/February 1989, pp. 24-25.

13 Ibid., p. 25.

14 Ibid.

15 Hendin, p. 152.

16 Ibid., p. 153.

17 Ibid.

18 In 1994, the U.S. state of Oregon passed Measure 16, which authorized a physician's prescription of lethal dosages. The law was prevented from going into effect until the ruling of the U.S. Supreme Court in *Quill and Glucksburg*. In 1997, the Oregon legislature introduced a referendum to void the statute. That referendum failed. However, in November of 1997 the Drug Enforcement Administration of the U.S. Department of Justice determined that it was against Federal regulations to prescribe controlled substances to kill. On February 26, 1998 the Oregon Health Services Commission authorized state funding of assisted suicide.

CHAPTER SIX

SOCIETY'S HISTORICAL REJECTION OF SUICIDE AND ASSISTED SUICIDE

- "Technological advances" are often used for justifying a "new" ethic regarding death. But the dependent have always been with us, and both the ability to withdraw assistance and the technology to kill have always been available.

- Contrary to popular belief, suicide and assisted suicide, though practiced, were not widely accepted in the ancient world.

- The death of Socrates, for example, is often cited as a model suicide. But Socrates (after whose cup of hemlock the Hemlock Society took its name) strongly condemned suicide. His death was actually an execution.

- While there were many documented suicides in ancient times — just as today — there were strikingly clear cultural "warnings" and prohibitions against suicide – just as today.

• Throughout its history, suicide has been condemned by Western civilization, and for good reason: it creates greater social dilemmas than it solves.

• Assisted suicide and other forms of euthanasia have a much stronger association with the primitive world, where there were no laws protecting the weak and vulnerable.

Advocates of euthanasia and assisted suicide often refer to it as a modern solution[1]; the next, logical step in "social progress;" or the "merciful" and "necessary answer" to "technological invasiveness and control." In reality, the idea is not new at all.

Primitive approach to problems

The growing acceptance of euthanasia does not mark a step toward progress and a "brave new world of freedom," but a very deliberate step back — back towards an admittedly more simple, primitive view of life and death. Unfortunately, this primitive view carries with it a certain barbarism, a certain disdain and personal fear of weakness, and at its heart, a regard only for the "productive human," with a disregard for the inherent value of human life.

Throughout Western history the issue of euthanasia and specifically assisted suicide has been debated, and the overwhelming conclusion has been to prohibit it. As Stephen Barker put it,

> The idea of respect for life has long been a
> central notion in the scheme of values of
> Western civilization. Despite many lapses

in practice — crimes committed showing contempt for life, sometimes on a terrifying scale — the idea of respect for life has continued to be regarded as affording a distinctive ideal standard, which many still believe sets much of Western civilization apart from other civilizations, whose ideals are perhaps less humane. This idea has informed Western attitudes concerning what is morally permissible and what ought to be legally permitted; especially so with regard to the conduct of medical practice.[2]

Respect for life an essential of Western civilization

Many cultures have toyed with the ethical acceptance of euthanasia. In some situations it was selectively accepted. In those cultures and sub-cultures that have embraced suicide and assisted suicide it has not been remembered as a "benefit," but as an "experiment" that reflected one of that society's darker expressions; a cold, expedient, and dangerous time in which to live. In many cases, of those societies that kept the practice, we remember the culture itself simply as "savage," or "brutal."[3] In most of these cultures, the individual is ultimately regarded as a mere cog in the larger social wheel.

This view is in stark contrast to the accepted moral hallmark of modern civilization and the Western concept of freedom, in which the individual is recognized as having intrinsic dignity and value. As Belgian physician Philipe Schepens puts it,

Throughout history freedom of the individual is based on the intrinsic *value* of the individual

> Euthanasia constitutes a major breach against the laws of humanity. It could in fact signify the abandoning of the very concept of democracy and relegate us to a new world and society which will be totalitar-

ian. A society in which people may dispose
of the very lives of others, where you have
to be declared fit by others to receive from
society the right to live. A society in which
the individual can exist only if he is wanted
by others, and who therefore ceases to have
absolute value. A society in which the weak
must yield to the stronger. This is more
than decadence. This is a gradual return
to the law of the jungle, to an animalistic
society where the survival of the fittest is
the rule.[4]

**A Viking
who died a
peaceful
death was
denied
entrance to
Valhalla**

Some views of death and suicide were
rooted in a cultural view that has little benefit
in our society. The Vikings, for example, believed only a violent death could get them into
Valhalla, or heaven. Death in battle was the
most coveted form, but suicide was grudgingly
seen as a reasonable alternative.[5] The ancient
nomadic Scythians saw suicide as a noble act
of the elderly or weakened, for it saved the other
members of the tribe the decision of carrying
or killing them. Many other societies and sub-
cultures, even into the twentieth century, have
accepted euthanasia as an answer for society's
problems. But using death as a way of deal-

**Barbarian
cultures
embraced
the
euthanasia
ethic**

ing with the physically or socially "problem-
atic" has always led to greater problems and
ultimately been condemned. Sadly, the condemnation is often heard only after the fact.
The eugenics movement of the 1920's and the
German euthanasia programs of the '30's and
'40's still cast an ominous shadow which euthanasia proponents scurry to avoid.[6]

Without exception, wherever euthanasia is
practiced it has offered a lingering dread and
distrust both in its "controlled practice" and
its "abuses."

Ancient history

The term "euthanasia" comes to us from the Greek, "eu-" meaning "good," and "-thanatos" meaning "death." But the term is a neologism, a newly-coined term; it was never used by the ancient Greeks to describe the modern concept of killing someone for benevolent motives. The noted translator J.M. Cooper states that no Greek philosopher ever discusses euthanasia in our contemporary sense of the word.[7]

Euthanasia **was not an ancient Greek term**

It is a modern "coining"

Today's euthanasia advocates often invoke suicide, and the abetting of suicide, as an accepted ancient practice, particularly in the Hellenic world. But while there is record of suicide in Greek history and literature, most historians concur that suicide in Greek culture was essentially held in disfavor.[8] There were many ancient laws against both suicide and assisted suicide. Even Socrates' evocative cup of hemlock, adopted as a symbol of self-determination by today's Hemlock society, was in fact an executioner's device, employed as punishment because of its general perception as a degrading death. Socrates himself condemned suicide, and accepted the hideous death only because he accepted his sentence.[9]

Greek culture held suicide in disfavor

It is a mistake to assume, as some do, that the appearance of suicide in the ancient manuscripts constitutes widespread acceptance of suicide by that culture. The fact that it was widely known does not mean that it was widely accepted.

A look at today's news, for example, reminds us that there are regular accounts of

**Appearance
of suicide in
Greek
literature
does *not*
mean it was
widely
embraced
by the
culture**

individual suicides as well as bizarre suicide cults. But the mere existence of these oft-reported suicides does not somehow constitute widespread social acceptance of the act. Despite those frequently reported events, suicide is still widely regarded with great disdain by our society. A researcher coming across these news stories hundreds of years from now would be seriously mistaken to conclude that suicide in today's culture does not carry a very strong taboo.

"But no," our researcher of the future might insist, "not only was it commonly practiced, but it appears regularly in their literature. They even made *Romeo and Juliet*, the story of a double suicide, required reading for young men and women in their formative years!"

What that future suicide advocate would miss – and what many of today's suicide advocates miss about the use of, and reference to, suicide in tragedy – is that they are *tragedies.*

**Tragedies
use suicide
as a plot
device, not
an
endorsement**

The use of suicide is a fairly common plot device, a literary tool of the tragic mode. Historically, the message of the tragic voice is to offer a life lesson in what human pitfalls the listener *should avoid,* not what should be emulated. Euthanasia advocates who cite the suicides mentioned in ancient manuscripts as some kind of sweeping cultural endorsement are being less than accurate about history.

The philosophers

Plato believed that suicide was generally cowardly and unjust,[10] that it represented abandonment of one's duty and violated divinely mandated responsibilities. From Plato's point of view it was an appropriate act only for those of immoral character or incorrigible behavior, and fitting only for those who had committed an inexcusably disgraceful act.[11] This was in keeping with the laws of Athens, which held that suicide was one of the *worst forms of death*, and therefore a most grievous form of punishment. In a startling display of ethnocentrism, an Athenian believed the only penalty considered more insufferable was being forced to continue living, forever banished from the city.

Plato

Suicide as an ignoble death

While Plato offered what was essentially a religiously based argument against suicide, Aristotle, in typical fashion, offered more "down-to-earth" reasons to condemn suicide. From his point of view, employing suicide is in essence taking the law into one's own hands, and unjustly deprives society of one of its members.[12]

Aristotle

The Stoics of the early Roman era emphasized the will of the individual above the good of the community, and believed that in general life should be lived to its utmost. They did believe that suicide could be permissible in certain rare instances when deprivation or illness no longer allowed for a "natural" life. But they did not maintain that suicide was justified whenever an indiviual lost the desire to live. And unlike modern advocates of assisted suicide, they esteemed nature's running its course as a better guide to sound judgment than an individual's transitory desires.[13]

Stoics

One of the reasons suicide was held in such disdain was that the Greeks saw self-mur-

der as an act as despicable as killing the closest member of one's family. Suicide commen-
tator A. Alvarez notes that the practice was,

> linked to the more profound Greek horror
> of killing one's own kin. By inference, sui-
> cide was an extreme case of this, and the
> language barely distinguishes between self-
> murder and the murder of kindred.[14]

Suicide illegal in Thebes and Athens

Suicide was condemned by the Pythagoreans, Sophocles, and Epictectus. The ancient laws of Athens and Thebes punished a man who committed suicide by denying him a conventional burial and confiscating his property. And since you cannot "prosecute" a corpse, in symbolic rejection, the Greeks would bury the body of a suicide outside of the city limits with the offending hand cut off.

The death of Socrates was not a suicide, but an execution which he accepted. Socrates strongly condemned suicide as did most Greeks. It was seen as the worst form of death. (Above, J.L. David's THE DEATH OF SOCRATES*)*

Social disdain for suicide is what discouraged suicide

In medieval times, a similar disdain was given the corpse of a suicide. At that time it was believed that suicidal inclinations were devilishly inspired, so the individual was presumed to have been possessed. In an effort to drive out the demon, a stake was driven through the corpse's heart and the body left at a rural crossroads.[15] (The medieval treatment of a suicide's corpse may coincidentally also have given rise to the legendary method of dispatching vampires by impaling the "possessed" corpse.)

An effective deterrent to "copycats"

"Copycat" suicides or suicide clusters have historically taken place in those circumstances in which society sends "mixed messages" regarding a suicide.[16] The clear disdain shown by communities of the Middle Ages and earlier cultures certainly must have made their mark, for few examples of suicide clusters are recorded from that era, while clusters do appear in those communities where suicide is "justified."

Jewish tradition

Since ancient times, Jewish and Christian philosophers have opposed suicide or abetting it as violations of both human good and duty towards God.

The scriptures and rabbinical teaching have held that suicide is a violation of God's order (Genesis 9:5). The Torah stongly con-

demns it. The book of Proverbs prescribes comfort, care, and pain medication for the dying
and depressed, not a speedy dispatch. "Give
strong drink to the dying, and wine to him with

Comfort for   a heavy heart."[17] It urges comfort, not death,
the dying,   for the depressed and afflicted; intervention
not death   and protection for those who are being drawn
toward death (Proverbs 24:11).

Josephus

In the first century, the Jewish historian
Josephus wrote that,

> suicide is alike repugnant to that nature
> which all creatures share... among the
> animals there is not one that deliberately
> seeks death or kills itself; so firmly rooted
> in all is nature's law — the will to live.

Usually suicidal thoughts are due to fears
associated with what an individual perceives
to be in the immediate future. Ironically,
Josephus himself was confronted with just
such a situation.

Surrounded by the Romans at Jotapata,
he unsuccessfully tried to talk the remnants
of the Jewish garrison into negotiating a surrender instead of killing themselves.

> What is it we fear that prevents us from
> surrendering to the Romans? Is it not
> death? And shall we then inflict upon our-
> selves certain death, to avoid uncertain
> death, which we fear, at the hands of our
> foes? ....In my opinion there could be no
> more errant coward than the pilot who, for
> fear of a tempest, deliberately sinks his
> ship before the storm.[18]

Old Testament

There are four cases of suicide recorded in the Old Testament, two are described as assisted suicides, and one is clearly a "copycat" suicide.

In one account (2 Samuel 1:1-15), Saul is killed by an Amelekite ally after pleading to be put out of his misery. This "kindness" is proudly reported back to Saul's troops. At the command of King David, for his act of dishonor the young man is executed on the spot . In another account, (1 Samuel 31:1-6) apparently before the Amelekite arrives on the scene, Saul appealed to his armor-bearer to assist him in suicide, but the terrified young man was unwilling. Saul then attempts to fall on his own sword. The desperate young man does the same.

Zimri (1 Kings 16:18-19) and Ahithophel (2 Samuel 17:23) die at their own hand. The perfidious Abimelech (Judges 9:50-56) dies in an assisted suicide.

In every case of suicide recorded in Scripture, the death represents a tragic end to a life that apparently did not meet with God's approval.[19] As in Greek tragedies, the death is seen as either a tragic or ignominious act.

Not only is this true of the several accounts of suicide in the Old Testament, it is also true of the New. The infamous death of Judas Iscariot (Matthew 27:3-10) and the apparent attempts at suicide found in the book of Revelation (Revelation 9:6) clearly indicate spiritual depravity. Finally, there is the scriptural story of a thwarted suicide, when Paul prevents his jailer from killing himself (Acts 16:25-29).

Suicide and Judeo-Christian scripture

The Greek tradition of eschewing suicide
and "assisted suicide" was summed up in the
Hippocratic Oath: "I will give no deadly medicine, even if asked, nor will I make a suggestion to this effect." The concept of dispatching
a patient was, even then, not new. It is clear
that Hippocrates, like many of the itinerant
doctors of his time, saw opportunities to "get
things over with," to clean up a messy situation, or get a problem out of the way. So much
could be "saved" by granting such a request.
But so much would be lost as well. There could
never be complete trust for a physician who
could kill as readily as he could heal.

**Christianity
embraced
the
Hippocratic
Oath**

Christianity

The rising new faith of Christianity ad-
mired and found itself in agreement with essential elements of the Oath, and though it had
not been quite universally applied in Greece,
with the rise of Christianity it became the ethical standard of the entire profession.[19]

Circa 400 A.D., St. Augustine's clear condemnation of suicide curbed a growing suicide
Augustine's cluster in North Africa, where a misguided sect
condemnation had equated suicide with martyrdom.[20] The
of suicide Circumcilliones, a devoutly active sect, sought
death so freely that they would jump from cliffs
as a fellow martyr died, in the hopes of shar-
ing in the "assured" sainthood. Only Augustine's declaration of the act as heretical brought
an end to the "suicide cluster."

By the thirteenth century Thomas Aquinas
had formulated Catholic teaching on suicide
in such a crystalline manner that it affected

all of Christianity through the Renaissance
and Reformation, and has echoed through
church teaching in subsequent centuries. He
taught that suicide violated one's duty to self,
the natural law of self-perpetuation, and one's
responsibilities toward other individuals and
society at large; it violated God's gift of life itself, and therefore God's authority over life.[21]

Philosphical thought

Secular social philosophers also noted
that society needed to protect the vulnerable
(including the medically vulnerable) from the
strong. In fact, for many philosophers it has
been precisely this regard for the weak that
separated a civilized culture from a savage one.

**Thomas
Hobbes**

In the early 1600's, the philosopher Thomas Hobbes described what he called the "social contract" that allowed people to live in a
civilized society. When mankind tried to live
outside of the "social contract" without its re-
strictions, in what he called the "state of nature," selfishness and confusion ruled. In that
more primitive world, the relentless — at times
ruthless — pursuit of one's own desires would
produce a culture in which each person would
live without any of the protective benefits of
society. One would live,

**Survival of
the fittest**

> worst of all, [in] continual fear, and dan-
> ger of violent death; and the life of man,
> solitary, poor, nasty, brutish, and short...[22]

Survival of the fittest reigned. This neatly
describes societies where the feeble are "dealt
with," and where the weak are eliminated "for

their own sake, and society's;" where it's "sink or swim" and "only the strong survive." Such a society does not reflect an advancement by man, but a reversion. It is clearly not a new concept, but a very old, and rejected one.

This expedient view of the weak and infirm can be dressed up and presented in a new way, but this "kind and simple approach" to difficult "social problems" still shows its primitive nature, even as today its proponents advance it as being in society's vanguard.

Hume   *Age of Reason*

In the sixteenth and seventeenth centuries philosophers began to challenge the dominant cultural prohibitions against suicide. John Donne and David Hume were two noted advocates. Hume's work, *On Suicide,* presented the above-mentioned "expedient approach" to human infirmities (very eruditely, of course). In his view, suicide could be good for the individual as well as society, and hence should be considered morally acceptable.

Donne

Donne's approach was different, and more guarded. His work, *Biathanatos,* was published after his death. In it he admitted to his own bouts with depression and suicidal thoughts.[23] He felt suicide was morally wrong in many cases. He also urged that society not change its laws against suicide as the laws often discouraged people from reverting to the practice. But he felt there could be some rare exceptions.

Donne, a Christian convert, advocated a position hauntingly similar to the heresy of the

Circumcilliones, the North African sect whose doctrine of suicide and martyrdom had been refuted by Augustine. They misguidedly spiritualized suicide as a quicker way to get close to God. Similarly, Donne felt that suicide might be acceptable if it was done with the intention of glorifying God.

While Donne was a voluminous writer of masterful essays and poetry, both sacred and secular, this was one work that was not widely revered.

John Locke

Other writers of the Age of Reason upheld and explained society's disdain for suicide. John Locke, who had such a profound effect on the Western view of democracy and freedom, and who had a formative influence on America's founders, argued that life, like liberty, represents an inalienable right which cannot be taken from, or given away by, an individual.[24]

Immanuel Kant, whose works also had a defining effect on modern democracy, argued that suicide was inconsistent with true personal freedom, or "autonomy." Liberty, according to Kant, does not mean the freedom to do whatever you want, but the ability to do what is right, or to follow the "categorical imperative,"

Kant

> Act in such a way that you treat humanity, whether *in your own person*, or the person of another, always at the same time as an end [in themselves] and never simply as a means.[25] [emphasis added]

Today's issue

From a social viewpoint, the arguments have largely remained the same. Modern philosophers have not departed from the essential elements of the debate, and in fact have offered few new insights. The debate has boiled down to this: while civilized society has held that it is morally permissible to allow a natural death (death from an underlying illness),

A natural death or euthanasia

it has frowned on killing to hasten or "clean up" the process. Much time is spent by modern euthanasia advocates in confusing the two types of death – a natural death and euthanasia – and in trying to convince society that "causing to die" is the moral equivalent of "allowing to die."

Once the confusion is maintained bewteen killing and dying, advocates like Dr. Joseph Fletcher (sometimes known as the "Father of Situational Ethics") can, with a straight face, propose that society "euthanize" disabled chil-

Fletcher

dren against their parents' wishes.[26] Without the distinction between comforting the dying and killing them, the Dutch program of euthanasia for the elderly and infirm can continue without hesitation, despite official governemnt reports that more than half of those killed made no such request.[27]

Civilization as we know it has on numerous occasions considered the case for assisted

Not a new issue

suicide. It has looked the issue straight in the eye and turned it away. The growing acceptance of euthanasia and moves to legalize "assisted suicide" do not mark a step toward progress and "a brave, new world" of freedom, but a very deliberate and calculated break with

the historic flow of civilized cultures. It is step-
ping back — back towards a more base and
morally "simple" life. The "law of the jungle"
has universally been recognized as antitheti-
cal to the civilized and kindly treatment of the
vulnerable and helpless; the elimination of the
weak has been an age-old trademark of barbarity, not civilization.

**Regressing
to barbarity**

NOTA BENE. In 1994, the U.S. state of Oregon passed
Measure 16, which authorized a physician's prescription of lethal dosages. The law was prevented from
going into effect until the rulings of the U.S. Supreme
Court in *Quill* and *Glucksburg.* In 1997, the Oregon
legislature introduced a referendum to void the statute. That referendum failed. However, in November
of 1997 the Drug Enforcement Administration of the
U.S. Department of Justice determined that it was
against Federal regulations to prescribe controlled
substances to kill. Then, on February 26, 1998 the Oregon Health Services Commission authorized state
funding of assisted suicide.

**An
American
epilogue**

On Thursday, March 26, 1998, an unnamed woman
in her mid-80's became the first known person to legally die under America's first physician-assisted suicide law. As in the Netherlands, all reporting of euthanasia in Oregon is voluntary, any submitted reports
are to be kept in secrecy, barred from public view.

NOTES

1 Hemlock literature, distributed in support of Oregon's Proposition 16.

2 Stephen Barker. I looked everywhere in an attempt to recover the origi-
nal source on this. Sorry Stephen; let me know and I will give you
credit.

3 Faberow cites the Polynesians, the Scythians, and the Vikings.

4 Dr. Ph. Schepens, Belgian physician, and General Secretary of the
World Federation of Doctors Who Respect Human Life, writing in
News Exchange, October, 1987. Reprinted in *Issues in Law and Medi-
cine*, Vol.3, No.4 1988[4]

5 A. Alvarez, *The Savage God (New York: Random House, 1971) p. 58.*

6 Derek Humphrey raises the spectre of Nazi euthanasia in a clumsy attempt to distance his proposals from theirs, "While the Nazi motives were barbarous, ruthless and unforgivable, the actual deaths were swift, though this is small consolation to the families of the killed;" and later, "It was a lapse by a section of the medical profession that must never be allowed to happen again." *Final Exit*, p.43.

7 J.M. Cooper, "Greek Philosophers on Euthanasia and Suicide," in *Suicide and Euthanasia*, ed. Brody, 14.

8 *When Death is Sought*, New York Task Force on Life and the Law, 1994.

9 Plato describes the death of Socrates in his work, *Phaedo*. Other than suicide, banishment from Athens was an alternative available to Socrates, but being a noble Athenian Socrates felt such punishment was a "fate worse than death."

10 Plato, *Laws*, Chapter 9, cited in *When Death is Sought*, p. 78.

11 Plato, *Phaedo* [Classic Texts version], p. 62

12 Aristotle, *Nichomachean Ethics*, 111, 1115 b7.

13 *When Death is Sought*, p. 79.

14 Alvarez.

15 Alvarez, quoted in Norman Faberow, *Suicide in Different Cultures* (Baltimore: University Park Press, 1975). The crossroads were apparently chosen for several reasons, as a public testimony for the passerby and

> "in the hope that the constant traffic would prevent the spirit from rising.... After the introduction of Christianity, the cross formed by the roads became a symbol which would disperse the evil energy concentrated in the dead body." (p. 11)

16 Loren Coleman, *Suicide Clusters* (Winchester, MA: Faber and Faber, 1987). See also "Manipulated Suicide" in this volume.

17 Alcohol is here used as a medication.

18 Josephus, *The Jewish War*, translated G.A. Williamson (London: Penguin Books, 1959), pp. 209-10.

Some Jewish rabbis have made the distinction of "kiddush ha-shem" ("sanctifying the divine name"). This is not suicide for self-interest, which is strongly condemned. Instead, the suicide seeks death to avoid being forced to commit a greater evil. The death of Samson; the seige of Masada; the four hundred children of the Talmud; and other stories of later Jewish tradition contain an element of this, "suicide for the sake of spiritual purity."

Josephus and other Jewish teachers presaged Augustine's refutation of "spiritualized suicide." According to this view, suicide is not an appropriate response to moral dilemma. If the expected evil to be suffered is not volitional, it is not an evil that can be attributed to the victim.

19 Faberow, p. ix.

20 The Circumcilliones and Donatists were accused of provoking non-believers to kill them. The primary objective appeared to be the avoidance of sin and avoiding further participation in a sinful world. Augustine's *City of God* vigorously condemned such theology as heretical. (Faberow, p. xiv.)

Incidentally, a similar religious heresy may also have given rise to the now-famous game, "Russian roulette." A cloistered Russian sect of the 1800's apparently used revolvers as a form of "casting lots." With one round in the multi-chambered cylinder, it was supposed that God would determine who was to live, and who could be ushered into the next life. Condemned as heretical; like most other suicide cults, it too died out. (Coleman, p. 99.)

21 Thomas Aquinas in Robert Wennberg, *Terminal Choices* (Grand Rapids, MI: Eerdmans, 1989), p. 66-71.

22 Thomas Hobbes, *Leviathan* (London: Penguin Books, 1973).

23 Faberow, xvi; and *When Death is Sought*, p. 80.

24 *When Death is Sought*, p. 81.

25 Immanuel Kant, *Grounding for the Metaphysics of Morals*, translated by J.W. Ellington (Indianapolis: Hackett, 1993).

26 Joseph Fletcher, "Elective Death," *Ethical Issues in Medine*, ed. Fuller Torrey (Boston: Little, Brown, 1968).

27 Richard Fenigsen, Report of the Dutch Government Committee on Euthanasia, *Issues in Law and Medicine* 7 (1991) 3.

CHAPTER SEVEN

"...EVEN IF ASKED..."

WHY DOCTORS SHOULD NOT KILL

> **If the physician presumes to take into consideration in his work whether a life has value or not, the consequences are boundless and the physician becomes the most dangerous man in the state.**
> –Dr. Christoph Hufeland (1762-1836)

• Euthanasia and physician-assisted suicide have been condemned throughout the history of medicine civilization . Although there have been lapses in this standard, society has recognized those lapses as ethical breaches.

• It has been suggested that new, technical advances "keep people alive longer" and that therefore modern physicians should embrace a new ethic. But the existence and endurance

of the **Hippocratic Oath** indicates that assisted suicide is in fact a very old issue, that
patients have been tempted to ask, and physicians tempted to comply, since the dawn of
written history.

• The ethical answer has always been to comfort, but not kill, a dying and vulnerable patient.

History has born out the wisdom of preventing doctors from being killers. The immediate
dangers include:

> • Undermining the trust of the doc-
> tor-patient relationship;

> • Patients would be less than hon-
> est about their illnesses if it might
> cost them their lives;

> • Risk of mistaken diagnoses;

> • Risk of coercion;

> • Immediate danger for the frail,
> disabled, and those unable to pay
> for beneficial medical care

> • Outside pressure on the physician,
> such as "cost cutting;"

> • For overworked doctors, killing
> would be much easier than continu-
> ously fighting a serious, chronic ill-
> ness.

- The American Medical Association has clearly stated, "Physicians must not perform euthanasia or participate in assisted suicide."

- In 1987 the World Medical Association (and in 1988 the British Medical Association) reviewed and reaffirmed their opposition to euthanasia.

- In 1996, the Federal Council of the Australian Medical Association rejected the practice by a vote of eighty to one.

The issue of doctors assisting in suicide is not a new one. The very difficult and emotional task of dealing with a dying patient, a patient in great pain, or the despondent and suicidal patient, has confronted the medical profession since it came into existence.

Hippocrates, sometimes known as the "Father of Medicine," wrote in the oath ascribed to him, "I will give no deadly medicine, *even if asked...*" It is clear that Hippocrates had either experienced or anticipated the pressure that would be brought to bear on physicians to use their healing knowledge to kill.

Hippocrates helped to establish many of the medical practices we today take for granted. He was meticulous in his direction to physicians, detailing the preparation of the operating room, care and use of implements, scrupulous cleanliness of the hands, use of splints, as well as general order and cleanliness. He insisted that the physician provide a restful place of the patient, with a cheerful surrounding, and that the doctor exercise conscientious "bedside manner." The physician, said Hippocrates, should be a man of honor, in good health, sympathetic and friendly, not self-seeking, temperate in eating and drinking, and a philosopher in outlook.[1] Hippocrates was less concerned with diagnosis than with prognosis, i.e., predicting the course of a disease and the possibility of cure or the likelihood of death.

Before Hippocrates appeared on the scene, Greek medicine had a decidedly primitive flavor, a strange mixture of religion, necromancy, and mysticism. Greek physicians were reputed to be skillful in dressing wounds and bandaging, while at the same time reciting incantations.[2] With Hippocrates, we come, as Sir William Osler puts it, "out of the murky night of the East, heavy with phantoms, into the bright daylight of the West." George Sarton adds,

> The main achievement of Hippocrates was the introduction of the scientific point of view and the scientific method to the cure of diseases. The importance of this can hardly be exaggerated. Hippocrates' personality, however shadowy, symbolizes one of the greatest initiatives in the history of mankind.[3]

It is the high ethical standards represented by the Oath – particularly the stricture against killing – which has elevated the physi-

Hippocrates set the standard for the profession

Hippocrates separated medicine, and our culture, from the savage world

cian to a place of honor in our culture. Without the ennobling Oath the doctor would easily be an agent of fear and suspicion. Anthro-
pologist Margaret Mead has studied the role
of the "medicine man" across cultures and
throughout history. She observes,

"It is society's job to protect the physician from such requests." -Margaret Mead

Throughout the primitive world the doctor and the sorcerer ended to be the same
person... He who had the power to cure
would necessarily be able to kill. Depending on who was paying the bill, the doc-
tor/witch doctor could try to relieve pain
or send the patient to another world. Then
came a profound change in the consciousness of the medical profession - made both
literal and symbolic in the Hippocratic
Oath: "...I will use treatment to help the
sick according to my ability and judgement, but never with a view to injury and
wrongdoing. Neither will I administer a
poison to anybody when asked to do so,
nor will I suggest such a course." For the
first time in our tradition there was a complete separation between killing and
curing...With the Greeks the distinction
was made clear. One profession...was to be
dedicated completely to life under all circumstances, regardless of rank, age, or in-
tellect–the life of a slave, the life of the
Emperor, the life of a foreign man, the life
of a defective child...

This is a priceless possession which we
cannot afford to tarnish... but society is
always attempting to make the physician
into a killer-to kill the defective child at
birth, to leave sleeping pills beside the bed
of the cancer patient...It is the duty of society to protect the physician from such
requests.[4]

It has been suggested that the oath was in
fact written by the Pythagoreans of the fifth

century B.C., and ascribed to Hippocrates at a later date. Whether authored by him or not, both Hippocrates and his Oath came to embody the definitive standard of ethical medicine. In the Roman world, both were widely honored. This was largely due to their championing by the leading physician of the time, Galen.

The essential message of the Oath, to "do no harm," is expressed in the Roman novel, *The Golden Ass*, by Apuleius, a contemporary of Galen. Through a poignant vignette Apuleius brings into sharp focus the physician's respect for life as being above and beyond the demands of the law. A doctor was asked for a fast-acting poison, allegedly "for a sick man in the throes of an inveterate, intractable disease who longed to escape the torture of his life," for at that time the Roman law was silent on the subject of suicide.[5] But in reality the poison was for the purpose of murdering the ostensibly ill man.

The physician sold a potion, but when later an innocent man was accused of murder, the physician revealed that he had actually sold a sleeping concoction, and not a deadly poison,

The clever physician

> because he did not believe it proper for his calling to be instrumental in bringing death to anybody, and because he had been taught that medicine had been invented not for the destruction of man but for his welfare.[6]

Aside from distrusting the buyer, the physician did not believe that his profession embraced poisoning, even for the sake of a "benevolent," self-inflicted act. The apparently dead man was awakened, the criminals punished and the physician rewarded.

As noted in the chapter on social ethics, with few exceptions, medical ethics has essentially retained its opposition to assisted suicide and commitment to the Hippocratic tradition down to the present day. The World Medical Association ratified what is known as the "Geneva Declaration" at an international conference in 1987. The modern Declaration is an adaptation of the Hippocratic Oath, and is still affirmed by the graduates of many modern medical schools. In light of this, says Dr. Owsei Temkin, "We see that in medical ethics the ancients not only preceded us but are very much with us."[7]

A dark chapter in the history of medical ethics

It is this ancient embrace of ethics which gives modern medicine its aura of character

One of the few exceptions to the widely held prohibition on physician-abetted death appears in 20th century Germany. And while this is commonly referred to as the Nazi Era, it is important to point out that the elimination of "unwanteds" began well before the Nazis came to power. The concept of "life devoid of value" or "life not worth living" was not a Nazi invention, it appeared in medical writing decades before Hitler came to power. Most influential was the book *The Release of the Destruction of Life Devoid of Value*, published in Leipzig in 1920. Its popularity is attested by the fact that two years later a second edition became necessary. The book advocated that the killing of "worthless people" be released from penalty and legally permitted. It was written by two prominent scientists, the jurist Karl Binding and the psychiatrist Alfred Hoche. Binding and Hoche speak of "absolutely worthless human beings"; they plead for "the killing of those who cannot be rescued and whose death is urgently necessary."

The widespread popularity of the book was offered as a defense of those magistrates and doctors tried in Nuremburg in 1948 for crimes against humanity.

Defense at Nuremburg

Those same trials at Nuremburg revealed much about the German campaign of human "medical experiments" and wholesale euthanasia. According to Dr. Leo Alexander one of the American investigators at the trials, it initially began as a selective cleansing of the "Aryan" population, targeting the mentally defective, psychotics, and those suffering from diseases of old age, including Parkinsonism, multiple sclerosis, and brain tumors. Even those with "involuntary depression" were dispatched, their brains then sent to neuropathologists for research.[8]

The apparent innocuousness of Germany's "small beginnings" is perhaps best shown by the fact that German Jews were at first excluded from the program. For it was originally conceived that "the blessing of euthanasia should be granted only to [true] Germans."[9] Dr. Alexander reports that the methods used and the personnel trained in the killing centers for the chronically sick became the nucleus for the much larger killing centers that were to be developed in the East, then ultimately applied to the Jews.

The "blessing" for "cleansing the race"

Sadly, the perpetrators cannot be dismissed as mere Nazi thugs. They were in fact from the highest strata of the intelligentsia, widely respected members of polite German society. According to Dr. Fredric Wertham, an expert on institutionalized violence,

Started by medical and academic leadership, then adopted by the Nazis.

The backbone of the whole project was the experts. It was their decision which sealed the fate of every victim. Who were these men? That is the most remarkable part of the story—and the most important one for the future of violence and, I believe, of mankind. They were not nonentities or outsiders. Most of them had all the hallmarks of civic and scientific respectability. They were not Nazi puppets, but had made their careers and reputations as psychiatrists long before Hitler came to power. Among them were more than twelve full professors at universities. Most of their names read like a roster of prominent psychiatrists. They have made valuable contributions to scientific psychiatry. They are still quoted in international psychiatric literature, which testifies to their scientific stature.

In addition to the professors of psychiatry, the experts included directors of large and well-known state hospitals from different parts of Germany, like Buch, near Berlin, and Eglfing, near Munich.... These experts were not new appointees of the Nazi regime, but had had long and honorable careers. They were by no means products of Nazism, but were parallel phenomena.[9]

Some people tried to avoid the question of responsibility for the Holocaust, dismissing it with the "great man" view of history. It was easier to blame Hitler as the single mad genius and creator of the evil, but the evidence makes it hard to dismiss the crimes as the product of a single, despotic mind. As Wertham points out,

> Hitler gave no order to kill mental patients indiscriminately. As late as mid-1940 (when thousands of patients had been killed in psychiatric institutions), Minister of Justice Guertner wrote to Minister Hans Lammers: "The Fuehrer has declined to enact a law [for putting mental patients to death]." There was no legal sanction for it.[11]

Dr. Alexander places the genesis of the Holocaust at the point at which the medical profession abandoned its ethical commitment to the vulnerable.

> The beginnings at first were merely a subtle shift in emphasis in the basic attitude of the physicians. It started with the acceptance of the attitude, basic in the euthanasia movement, that there is such a thing as life not worthy to be lived. This attitude in its early stages concerned itself merely with the severely and chronically sick. Gradually the sphere of those to be included in this category was enlarged to encompass the socially unproductive, the ideologically unwanted, the racially unwanted and finally all non-Germans.
>
> But it is important to realize that the infinitely small wedged-in lever from which this entire trend of mind received its impetus was the attitude toward the non-rehabilitable sick.[12]

Attitude of physicians

Continued on Page Two.   Continued on Page Twenty.

Nazis Plan to Kill Incurables to End Pain; German Religious Groups Oppose Move

By The Associated Press.

BERLIN, Oct. 7 —The Ministry of Justice in a detailed memorandum explaining the Nazi aims regarding the German penal code today announced its intention to authorize physicians to end the sufferings of incurable patients.

The memorandum, still lacking the force of law, proposed that "it shall be made possible for physicians to end the tortures of incurable patients, upon request, in the interests of true humanity."

This proposed legal recognition of euthanasia—the act of providing a painless and peaceful death—raised a number of fundamental problems of a religious, scientific and legal nature.

The Catholic newspaper Germania hastened to observe:

"The Catholic faith binds the conscience of its followers not to accept this method of shortening the sufferings of incurables who are tormented by pain."

In Lutheran circles, too, life is regarded as something that God alone can take.

A large section of the German people, it was expected in some interested circles, might ignore the provisions for euthanasia, which

overnight has become a widely-discussed word in the Reich.

In medical circles the question was raised as to just when a man is incurable and when his life should be ended.

According to the present plans of the Ministry of Justice, incurability would be determined not only by the attending physician, but also by two official doctors who would carefully trace the history of the case and personally examine the patient.

In insisting that euthanasia shall be permissible only if the accredited attending physician is backed by two experts who so advise, the Ministry believes a guarantee is given that no life still valuable to the State will be wantonly destroyed.

The legal question of who may request the application of euthanasia has not been definitely solved. The Ministry merely has proposed that either the patient himself shall "expressly and earnestly" ask it, or "in case the patient no longer is able to express his desire, his nearer relatives, acting from motives that do not contravene morals, so request."

NEW YORK
TIMES,
October 8,
1933

The Nazis authorized what some physicians already embraced, but even to the end of the war, euthanasia was never officially legalized.

Why doctors should not kill

While individuals like Jack Kevorkian have pushed for "physician-assisted suicide," others have suggested that if assisted suicide is legalized the medical community should be prohibited from doing it. Some members of the Hemlock Society oppose doctor involvement because they believe individuals themselves, and not paternalistic physicians, should make the final decision.[13]

But there are also some who would grudgingly accept assisted-suicide but oppose physician involvement. It would be beneath doctors. Another profession, "obitrist," would do the job, as it is viewed as messy and unseemly. It would "sully" the medical profession. Author Maggie Gallagher offered a similar argument in a widely published editorial.

> Making it the responsibility of doctors to kill patients is a form of barbarism not seen since the Dark Ages, when barbers both cut hair and performed surgery, because both acts require the use of a knife.... If we are no longer willing to protect the sanctity of all human beings, let us at least keep, as one small saving grace, the honor and dignity of the medical profession intact.[14]

While this is a valid observation – that the honorable profession should not be violated – the emphasis is misplaced. It misses the deeper and more pressing issue. Doctors should be kept from killing, because of all professions, they are the most able and the most likely.

The practice of assisting in a suicide would sully any profession. Many professionals would be strikingly tainted by requiring them to kill - ballet dancers, school teachers, geologists. *But it is doctors who by profession are prohibited from killing, and for one simple reason, they are best positioned to do so.* And they are the most likely to be tempted; without that brightly shining ethical guideline, they most surely would be pressured to do so.

In the United States, professional medical organizations have entered the debate on

Doctors have the most occasion to kill, and all the best "reasons"

assisted suicide and euthanasia. Their official positions reflect the age-old rule that the physician not cause death, (*Primum non nocere*: "The first thing is not to harm.") The American Medical Association, the American College of Physicians, and the American Geriatrics Society all distinguish assisted suicide and euthanasia from the withdrawing or withholding of treatment, and from the provision of pain control medication or other medical care that may risk fatal side effects.[15] Doctors and nurses are even prohibited from participating in a state-mandated execution.

Protecting the doctor from outside pressure

Why was the Oath protective for the physician? It would allow them to resist the pressure of others. After all, without an ethical contract between physician and patient, a doctor might be considered simply an employee and the relationship purely business. If the patient is merely the employer, the request for death – whether motivated by fear of the unknown, or pain, or depression – could cloud the attending doctor's thinking and blur the distinction between the employer/employee relationship and the doctor/patient relationship.

The physician as an employee

Perhaps more ominous, if the physician is being paid by a third party, perhaps an heir; perhaps an enemy; perhaps a financially strapped HMO, that employer/employee relationship and the promise of personal gain would, without the prohibition on killing, leave the medical profession open to accusations of being "hitmen with scalpels."

Destroying the "evidence"

The Oath has also helped physicians avoid the temptation to "cover their tracks." If a doctor misdiagnosed, or botched a treatment, a swift dispatch of the "suffering" individual would give the appearance of kindness to an otherwise messy situation. In ancient times, a family's revenge – or in today's world, the threat of malpractice – could motivate an unscrupulous practitioner to bury their errors under the guise of compassion.

Possible use as a cover - up

Misdiagnosis

Leaving the unscrupulous aside, even conscientious doctors can be wrong. It is extremely difficult to correctly prognose that a patient has six months or less to live. Yet this is the often-suggested guideline set out in proposed assisted suicide laws. Once the request for death is acted on, any misdiagnosis or incorrect prognosis would be irrelevant.

"Oops."

Euthanasia would ease the work load

A doctor's life is a demanding one. For many overworked physicians, the temptation to relieve the pressures involved in the continuous fight against chronic illness would be palpable. Gently easing a depressed and chroni-

**Used to
relieve
stress – the
physician's**

cally ill patient "out of their misery" could
easily be justified if there were few barriers
against it. And hard to resist if widely practiced by others.

Removes emotional barriers

The use of medicine to assist a suicide
removes some of the natural psychological
barriers to the act. Many who can not bring
themselves to the finality of self-slaughter because of its violence are more receptive to taking a pill, without facing the full implications
of the act. As suicide expert Alfred Alvarez
points out,

> Modern drugs not only make suicide more
> or less painless, they have also made it
> seem magical. A man who takes a knife
> and slices deliberatively across his throat
> is murdering himself. But... swallowing
> sleeping pills he seems not so much to be
> dying as merely seeking oblivion for
> awhile.[16]

**A doctor's
involvement
would
encourage
the
tentatively-
suicidal**

The psychological barrier is even more
dramatically removed if the "suicidal" act is
actually done by another. And how much more
so if that other is a doctor, who simply offers it
as an alternative treatment? The physician's
expertise would ease the trepidation of an otherwise reluctant patient.

A doctor is dispassionate by training

We must also recognize that without some external, "higher authority" defining right and wrong, the trained physician could easily grow cold and dismissive of the unique human life that lies in his or her trust.

Remember, the effective doctor is trained to be dispassionate - cool, calm, and collected under pressure. This detached, clinical approach to the human body has saved many lives, and at critical moments. The routine knowledge of anatomy, coupled with a mind uncluttered by emotion, allows for swift and effective action. But there is a "flip side" to this training; without ethical guidelines this detachment can carry a very high price.

Cold and calculating

"When a doctor does go wrong he is the first of criminals. He has nerve and he has knowledge."
Sherlock Holmes (A.Conan Doyle)
in *The Speckled Band*

Doyle refers here to the fictitious Dr. Roylott, who is using his extensive knowledge in an attempt to secure a legacy. But Holmes continues his observation, "Palmer and Pritchard were among the heads of their profession." He refers here to two actual murderers, notorious turn-of-the-century physicians, both of whom were hanged for their clever crimes. Doyle himself was trained as a doctor at the University of Edinburgh; he personally understood the importance of the physician's Oath.

Doyle recognized the dangers posed to society if the specialized training of the physician were used by individuals that did not adhere to a clear moral code which keeps that knowledge in check.

If a physician does leave the historic and clearly hewn path of proper conduct, the results can be ominous indeed. He can use the trust and training bestowed on him in a way that few others can. He knows precisely how to kill quickly and efficiently. He knows how to camouflage a death to make it look natural, or like an accident, or perhaps ... a suicide.

NOTES

1 Owsei Temkin, "The Idea of the Respect for Life in the History of Medicine," *Respect for Life* (Baltimore: Johns Hopkins, 1976), p. 2.

2 Ibid.

3 George Sartin quoted in Harding, "Great Physician," *Great Men of Science.* Harvard 1971

4 Margaret Mead, "The Physician," *Journal of Ethnography* 3, no. 1, 1937.

5 Not only the Romans, but many later legal systems dropped punishment for suicide. Prosecutors sometimes feel silly punishing a corpse; and unsuccessful suicides were better helped by compassionate intervention, as opposed to prosecution. See Kamisar.

6 Apuleius, *Metamorphoses*, quoted in Temkin.

8 Temkin.

9 Leo Alexander, "Medical Science under Dictatorship," *New England Journal of Medicine* 241:39-47, 1949. (Reprinted in Horan and Mall's excellent text, *Death, Dying, and Euthanasia*, from University Publications of America. **Highly recommended.**)

10 Defendant Viktor Brack, Chief Administrative Officer in Hitler's private chancellory, so testified at the Nuremberg Medical Trial, *1 Trials of War Criminals Before the Nuremberg Military Tribunal Under Control Council Law* No. 10, 877-80 (1950) ("The Medical Case") Quoted in Kamisar.

11 Fredric Wertham, *A Sign For Cain*, (New York: Macmillan, 1966) and reprinted in Horan and Mall.

12 Ibid., p.615

13 Humphry, *Final Exit*, pp. 91-94.

14 Maggie Gallagher, "Is it a Right to Die or a Right to Kill?" Universal Press Syndicate, March 1996.

15 The Council on Ethical and Judicial Affairs of the American Medical Association. Also stated in the American College of Physicians Ethics Manual," 3rd ed., *Annals of Internal Medicine* 117 (1992).

16 Alfred Alvarez, *The Savage God* (New York: Random House, 1971) p.124

CHAPTER EIGHT

TARGET AUDIENCE: THE VULNERABLE, THE DEPRESSED, THE DESPAIRING

Target: the elderly

Perhaps the group at greatest risk of manipulated suicide and euthanasia is the elderly. Due to a variety of social factors, the elderly is already the social group with the greatest per capita rate of suicide.

With retirement and aging often come a reduction in income, loss of mobility, and a vulnerable dependence on others. Despite popular misconceptions, less money is spent on medical treatment for the elderly than other ages, and in comparison to their juniors, the elderly are less likely to have their depression and psychological needs treated. Finally, the soaring incidence of elder abuse indicates that this segment of our society is particularly vulnerable to deadly abuse and manipulation.

Story of Gerald Klooster

Gerald Klooster had a long and successful career as a California physician. But after retirement in 1989 it was discovered that he was suffering from Alzheimer's. He slowly grew incompetent and by 1995 he lived a life dependent on others, particularly his wife Ruth.

Then in September of 1995 his son, Dr. Gerald "Chip" Klooster II, discovered that his mother had joined the pro-euthanasia Hemlock Society, made a "shopping list" of lethal drugs, and contacted Jack Kevorkian to see if he would help her husband die. Various family members filed for emergency custody of the senior Klooster. A court battle ensued. In November, sensing imminent danger, Chip spirited his father to his Michigan home.

Wife joins Hemlock, calls Kevorkian

In June of 1996 the senior Klooster was returned to California after a long and costly court battle that drew national attention. Within three months of being returned to his wife's care, Gerald was found on his kitchen floor having ingested a near-fatal combination of alcohol and sleeping pills (a favorite Hemlock formula). The Alameda county sheriff characterized it as "an attempted suicide with suspicious circumstances." Chip's observations would lend credence to that view, "My father is incapable of physically taking his own medicine."[1]

Suspicious "suicide"

On January 23, 1997, Chip Klooster was initially granted custody. But the legal wrangling continued, with the elder Klooster seemingly oblivious to the circumstances. Ultimately, a jumble of decisions led to Chip's sister having legal custody but the elder Klooster returning home to live with his wife. The judge insisted on a long list of protective conditions including a live-in attendant, the barring of alcohol and all other drugs from the home, and a prohibition on Ruth taking her husband out of state without the daughter's authorization.

Chip's attorney said there was little his client could do to block his father's return to his mother's home. "But we appear to have had some effect today," he said. "The thing that will make us most happy is if he lives a long and happy life."[2]

Dr. Klooster's plight is a glimpse at the incredible pressures that are mounting on the vulnerable aged. The elderly are more easily manipulated than when they enjoyed their salad days; there are elements within our culture which would seek to expedite their departure.

Family members leery of father's 'suicide' try

By Martha Irvine
Associated Press

CASTRO VALLEY – An Alzheimer's patient whose son feared he was being pushed by other family members to kill himself with Dr. Jack Kevorkian's help remained hospitalized Wednesday after apparently ... on sleeping pills and whiskey. ... are investig...

have anything to indicate a crime was committed, but there are many unanswered questions."

Alameda County Superior Court Judge William McKinstry issued an emergency order returning care and custody back to daughter Kristen Hamstra, who is Klooster's conservator. He had been living with his wife, Ruth, since June in their Castro ... home.

"I'm in shock. ... All I can say is I told everybody this was going to happen," said the Kloosters' physician son, Chip, who took his father to his Petoskey, Mich., home last year after learning that his mother had contacted Kevorkian.

A custody dispute lasted nine months until a judge ordered Klooster returned to his daughter's home in Discovery Bay and then to his wife's home. The reunited co...

Craig Klooster, the couple's oldest son, said his mother was too upset to speak with reporters. He also said the family resented the Sheriff's Department investigation.

"We're in the media one more time wh... we shouldn't be, when we don't want to b... he said in a shaking voice. "It's very sad."

Chip Klooster said a doctor told him h... father had swallowed about 100 pills ... three times a lethal dose – a...

...ble of physically tr...

SACRAMENTO BELL
September 26, 1996

Myth of costly health-care

The "growing cost of healthcare" is one of the oft-cited reasons offered for reducing the value our society has traditionally placed on the lives of the elderly. This "growing burden" is often cited for enacting sweeping change in the way we care for the dependent elderly or disabled.

Richard Lamm, former Colorado Governor and presidential candidate, created a stir when he publicly announced that the elderly and handicapped had a duty to die and get out of the way. Though challenged on this he has reiterated his position, stating, "There is not enough money, and we can buy an incredible amount of health if we utilize our resources better."[3]

President Clinton raised a similar suggestion while discussing his revolutionary health plan, "There are a lot of extra costs" toward the end of life, he told Tom Brokaw, "having more Americans sign living wills is one way to weed them out."[4] An observant reporter pointed out, "But the purpose of the living will is to give patients more autonomy, not to die early and save money for a fiscally-strapped government."[5]

Lamm and Clinton: save money with change in long-term medical care for the elderly and vulnerable

Already getting less

But the real facts about elders and health care are quite startling. Older people are already much less likely to get aggressive, high-cost and often futile medical care towards the end of their lives than is commonly believed, according to a study by the Alliance for Aging Research. According to the Alliance director, Daniel Perry, there is an unsubstantiated image in the popular mind of "very ill, very old people at the end of life, consuming more than their fair share of Medicare dollars." [6] But it is simply not true.

Myth of higher cost

The study, done in conjunction with the Open Society Institute's Project on Death in America, found that of the "Seven Deadly Myths" about the last year of life, the number one misconception is that older people commonly receive heroic, high-tech treatments at the end of life. In fact, fewer than half of all people over sixty-five die in the hospital. And the older people are, the less likely they are to receive aggressive care when dying.

Not futile treatment

According to the chairman of the study, Dr. Gene Cohen, in those cases when the elderly do receive aggressive care it is not necessarily futile. Many get to live longer, enjoyable lives, and it is extremely difficult for doctors to predict who is really terminally ill or on the brink of death.[7]

The elderly and the poor; the last in line

But not only is the pervasive image of "futile, costly treatment for the elderly" untrue, it has tended to justify the actual reduction of care and medical intervention for the aged. In what is recognized as the most comprehensive study of its kind, The New England Medical Center found that for many people, the medical care provided to HMO members is adequate. But they found some glaring exceptions, the elderly and the poor were consistently under-treated. For monetary reasons it is easier to minimize treatment of patients with serious and chronic illnesses

HMO's and the elderly

The six-year study found that the elderly and chronically-ill poor who belonged to HMOs were much less likely to be treated in hospitals or to see physician specialists, spent less time with doctors during office visits and received less intensive treatment.[8] John Ware, one of the authors of the study, commented that previous health studies had failed to focus on chronically-ill elderly and poor patients, yet, "this is the group for whom health care matters the most."

A separate study which appeared in the *Journal of the American Geriatric Society* found that seriously ill elderly patients are much less likely to undergo surgery and other costly treatment than younger patients. Patients eighty and older underwent surgery about half as often as under-fifty patients with the same illness, and their hospital bills averaged about $7,000 less. The sharp difference in treatment based on age held up even after researchers accounted for differences in the patients' severity of illness and treatment preferences.[9]

Elderly already receive fewer operations

Elder abuse

But the elderly population does not suffer only at the hands of the medical bureaucracy.

Increased attention is being given to the problem of elder abuse. Elder abuse comes in various forms – physical; emotional; financial or fiduciary; neglect; self-neglect; and abandonment. Institutional neglect or outright physical abuse is already well-recognized and has become increasingly common in the last two decades of the twentieth century, but it is easier to spot. Domestic abuse is also widespread and much more difficult to detect.

Domestic abuse

Elder abuse soaring

From 1986 to 1994 there has been a steady increase in the reporting of domestic elder abuse nationwide, slowly climbing from 117,000 reported cases in 1986 to 241,000 cases in 1994, a 106% increase. But these are only the reported cases, and domestic elder abuse often goes unobserved. Excluding self-neglecting elders, researchers estimate there were 820,000 cases of domestic elder abuse in 1994, and with self-neglecting elders added, the total number of abuse cases was estimated at 1.86 million for that year.[10]

Assisted suicide, a parallel phenomenon, or the ultimate abuse?

It is significant that in the vast majority of "assisted suicide" cases involving the elderly, the strongest supporter of suicide and the most likely "assistant" is a spouse or other close family member. Statistics have shown that – as in the case of most murders – the individual most likely to harm a vulnerable elder is in fact, not a stranger, but their closest relative or caregiver. Assisted suicide may prove to be the ultimate form of elder abuse.

One type of elder abuse identified by researchers is termed "reversed spousal abuse."[11] This form of abuse occurs when the victims of long-term abuse find themselves responsible for taking care of the daily basic needs of disabled abusers and choose to retaliate with direct physical abuse or neglect.

Spousal abuse

Another more common form of abuse occurs due to the psychological pressures of caring for chronically or terminally ill family members. It is suggested that the aggressive behavior is a result of "psychological density."[12] In other words, the emotions of the situation slowly build beyond the caregiver's capacity. In these cases patient and caregiver are very dependent on each other with no outlet for their feelings, needs, or frustrations. Moreover, the longer the chronic illness lasts, the greater the danger that the couple will become isolated through their own disengagement as well as that of their social network.

Isolation and discouragement of caregiver and patient contribute to abuse situations

Intervention, and respite care needed

This pattern also reveals itself in many, if not most, assisted suicide cases. The caregiver, usually a spouse, acquiesces to the frustration and emotional strain of the loved one's illness or disability. This is precisely the scenario suggested by "manipulated suicide" commentators. What is needed in both cases – elder abuse and the ultimate abuse of assisted suicide – is intervention and the dynamic involvement of

Assisted "suicide" often the result of emotional strain

other caring individuals.

The aging population

The pressures on the elderly will only grow. The elderly population increased eleven-fold from 1900 to 1994; the under-sixty-five population just three-fold. The number of centarians – those one hundred years or older – more than doubled from 1980 to 1995. Four in five were women.

The existing social pressure on the elderly population will grow exponentially in the coming century, with the ratio of elderly people to working-age people (age 20-64) doubling between 1990 and 2050.

Target: the disabled

It only takes a brief perusal of Jack Kevorkian's patient list to realize that the debate over the "right to die" has nothing to do with those who are dying, for few of his victims could accurately have been called "terminal." As Kevorkian told NBC's *Dateline*, in explaining the killing of Judith Curren (according to the medical examiner Curren had no signs of terminal illness), "She was incapacitated. She was in a wheelchair. She'd lie in bed. She was in pain....It had nothing to do with lethality. It's quality of life."[13]

"It's quality of life." - Jack Kevorkian

Euthanasia advocates are usually somewhat vague about exactly what they mean by the "quality of life," but invariably the disabled fall into the realm of doubt. This was most dramatically demonstrated in the case of

Elisabeth Bouvia of Riverside, California. Elisabeth suffered quadriplegia due to cerebral palsy but nevertheless she had faced the challenges of life. She earned a Bachelor's at University of California, Riverside. She courted and married. She desired to be a counselor to other paraplegics so pursued, and essentially earned, a master's degree in psychology.

Elisabeth Bouvia

But then in 1983 the tide changed. The all-important final-semester internship was denied her because the hospital – which had signed her on as a counselor for the disabled – hadn't known that she was herself disabled. They would not accommodate her. Other things snapped. Her mother committed suicide. Her brother died. She went through a miscarriage. Her marriage dissolved.

Things fell apart

She was without emotional moorings and checked herself into the county hospital. There she asked them to help her die. She had no terminal condition, and physically she had the same limitations with which she had four years earlier faced the world, conquered college, and found love. But she was emotionally on the edge and couldn't handle her personal setbacks. The hospital said that they would care for her, but they would never oversee her intentional death.

That was enough for civil libertarians intent on "equal justice." If she wanted to "go over the edge" they were committed to helping her. After a long court battle the A.C.L.U. ultimately won an appeals court decision which would have forced the hospital to participate in dispatching Elisabeth. There was just one problem. Elisabeth didn't really want to die.

She changed her mind

She, like most depressed and confused

suicide candidates, was seeking affirmation and intervention through her appeal for "help in suicide." In fact, psychologists have always recognized that such a request is a cry for help. Ten years after the fact, the precedent of the appeals decision still stands, and is often cited by Hemlock lawyers.[14] But ironically Liz Bouvia decided to live, having received the attention and intervention she had actually sought.[15]

The disabled are particularly vulnerable to the siren's song of "assisted suicide" and will be a target community in those jurisdictions in which it is authorized. Physical circumstances as well as society seem to subtly conspire against them.

Physical links to depression

Physical exercise, which is taken for granted by "normal people," promotes the body's production of emotionally invigorating endorphins. These naturally occurring "shots in the arm" are much more difficult for the average disabled person to acquire. The pleasant lift after a brisk stroll to the mailbox, or a walk upstairs is not often experienced if you're bedridden or in a wheelchair.

The disabled are physically more susceptible to depression

Science has also discovered that factors such as exposure to sunlight and long months of inactivity affect the levels of a substance called seratonin, which is found in our brains. Seratonin is a neurotransmitter, low levels of which have been directly linked to chronic depression, and suicidal thoughts. In addition to the effects of physical inactivity, individuals who are disabled through accident or sudden illness must also wrestle with the emotional pain of knowing how they used to live.

"Superman doesn't live here anymore."

Actor Christopher Reeve, well known for portraying the title role of "Superman" in several Hollywood hits, suffered a tragic accident in 1995. While riding competitively, his horse suddenly stopped, propelling the actor head-first over the animal's head.Reeve broke his neck and is now quadriplegic.

In an interview with ABC News' *20/20* several months later, Reeve admitted that he had battled severe depression, particularly when the full realization of his vulnerable condition hit him. Like many others in similar circumstances, he faced suicidal depression.

Reeve battled suicidal depression

"Maybe I should just check out," was a dominant thought, he said. It was his wife Dana that helped him snap out of it. "You are still you inside," she told him, "and I love you." His children also were a central part of restoring his positive attitude, reinforcing again what thousands of depressed and dependent individuals tell us - it is critically important for the family to shower love and unqualified support on the suicidally depressed.

But it is not just a one-shot experience. "The first two months were the worst," Reeve told Barbara Walters. "The demons would haunt me in the middle of the night, particularly between two and seven a.m." The loneliness and isolation of their condition leaves the disabled continually vulnerable to depression.

**Family
support and
encouragment
critical**

Fortunately, Reeve was victorious in the battle
with depression, but it was "as the love and
support of family and friends came to me."

The disabled: a wake-up call

The disability rights community is wak-
ing up to the impending threat posed by cul-
turally accepted assisted suicide.   Diane
Coleman is the co-founder of "Not Dead Yet,"
established to fight the federal appeals court
rulings which granted the terminally ill and
disabled the right to assisted suicide
(*Glucksburg* and *Quill*). According to Coleman,
"A public policy that says, 'You have such mis-
erable lives as a group, we as a society understand why you want to die,' is a dangerous
public policy."[16]

**Public
policy
aimed at
disabled**

On March 24, 1997, the National Council on Disability issued a position paper, "Assisted Suicide: A Disability Perspective." That
paper concluded,

**Danger of
rationing**

> The dangers of permitting physician-as-
> sisted suicide are immense. The pressures
> upon people with disabilities to choose to
> end their lives, and the insidious appro-
> priation by others of the right to make that
> choice for them are already prevalent and
> will continue to increase as managed care
> and limitations upon Health Care re-
> sources precipitate increased "rationing"
> of Health Care services and health care
> financing.
>
> People with disabilities are among
> society's most likely candidates for ending
> their lives, as society has frequently made
> it clear that it believes they would be bet-
> ter off dead, or better that they had not

been born. The experience in the Netherlands demonstrates that legalizing assisted
suicide generates strong pressures upon
individuals and families to utilize that
option, and leads very quickly to coercion
and voluntary euthanasia. If assisted suicide were to become legal, the lives of
people with any disability deemed too difficult to live with would be at risk, and
persons with disabilities who are poor or
members of racial minorities would likely
be in the most jeopardy of all.[17]

Minorities

As mentioned, the elderly and poor are
already much less likely to get adequate treatment. Physicians who are active in delivering
Health Care to minority communities are also
concerned what this would mean for their patients.

A study published in the Detroit Free
Press found that many blacks were fearful that
white doctors will "pull the plug" on black
patients much sooner than on whites in their
care. "There is a lot of suspicion," said researcher Annette Dula, "People know they
don't get the healthcare they need when they
are living. What's to make them think anything
will be different if they are dying?"

Dr. Nicholas Carballeira, Director of
Boston's Latino Health Institute said this when
asked about legalizing assisted suicide,

> In the abstract it sounds like a wonderful
> idea, but in a practical sense it would be a
> disaster. My concern is for Latinos and
> other minority groups that might be dis-
> proportionately counseled to opt for phy-
> sician assisted suicide.[18]

**Minorities
or
unpopular
groups the
most likely
candidates**

Whether it be the elderly, the disabled, or those with serious and apparently incurable illnesses like AIDS; there is within every society a sizable number of individuals who are dependent on the empathy, compassion, and involvement of others. These are the ones at greatest risk of "assisted suicide." They are also the target audience in the current attempt to market the idea of "self-deliverance."

Implicit in the push to legalize assisted suicide is that, at its heart, it is not meant for those whom we care for, but for those whom we no longer care for.

NOTES

1 "Each year in the United States, over 6,000 people aged 65 years and older take their own lives.... No single factor... places an older person at greater risk than psychiatric illness." Yeates Conwell, PhD. American Suicide Foundation White Paper, 1996.

2 Martha Irvine, Associated Press Wire Story, *Sacramento Bee*, September 9, 1996. A4

3 Sabin Russell, *San Francisco Chronicle*, February 8, 1997. A17

4 Richard Lamm, "The Ten Commandments of Health Care," *The Humanist*, May/June 1987.

5 Interview with Tom Brokaw, *NBC Special on Health Care Reform*, November, 1993.

6 Joseph Shapiro, *US News and World Report*, April 4, 1994.

7 "Study: Elderly Less likely to Get Costly Care," Reuters, May 5, 1997.

8 Dr. Gene Cohen, director of the Center of Aging, Health and Humanities at George Washington University. Cited in Reuters.

9 *Los Angeles Times*, October 2, 1996, p. 1.

10 *Journal of the American Geriatric Society*, September 1996, as reported in the *Washington Post*, September 10, 1996, Health section, pg. 5.

11 "Elder Abuse in Domestic Settings,"*Report of the National Council on Elder Abuse*, 1994.

12 Sengstock (1991), reported in the *Research Digest of the National Council on Elder Abuse* (NCEA), Vol. 3, No.1, University of Delaware, 1996.

13 Kruse (1986), as reported in *Research Digest of the National Committee on Elder Abuse* (NCEA) Vol. 3 No.1, Spring 1996.

14 *Dateline* interview; NBC, 8/12/96

15 Ignoring Liz's other incredible emotional challenges, Judge Lynn Compton reduced her situation to only her physical condition. Since she was "condemned ... to continued existence in her helpless and to her, intolerable condition ... (she had) the right to enlist assistance from others, including the medical profession, in making death as painless and quick as possible." And "the medical profession had a duty" to assist in that request.

16 As of this writing (1998) Elizabeth still lives in southern California.

17 Cox News Service article in *San Francisco Examiner*, 11/7/96. A11.

18 Published by the National Council on Disability, an independent federal agency whose twenty members are appointed by the President and confirmed by the Senate. Reprinted in "Life at Risk," NCCB Secretary for Pro-Life Activities. Washington D.C.

But it is not just the physically disabled who are at risk. Those who are mentally, emotionally, or physically impaired to the degree that they need others to make decisions for them are perhaps in the most danger. The Dutch government has documented involuntary and non-voluntary acts of euthanasia, but contemporary American courts have been just as ruthless in disregarding the vulnerable nature of the incapacitated. In the startling *Glucksberg* decision of the U.S. Ninth Circuit Court of Appeals, Judge Stephen Reinhardt writes,

Finally, we should make it clear that a decision of a duly appointed surrogate decision maker is for all legal purposes the decision of the patient himself.

CHAPTER NINE

MANIPULATED SUICIDE

One of the greatest dangers posed by legalizing assisted suicide is the subtle pressures it would bring to bear on the vulnerable. Can individuals be persuaded to accept suicide even if they would not have considered it on their own? Oh, yes; history is very clear on that. And if the climate is right, the persuasion would be – and has been – quite easy.

Persuasion is sometimes easy

Mass suicide

But can the power of suggestion be enough to convince an individual to take one's life? Ominously, the subtle, "herd mentality" is even capable of leading whole groups of people into blithely accepting an unnecessary death. On March 26, 1997, thirty-nine indi-

viduals who "appeared very upbeat and expressed pleasure that they were going to a better place" committed suicide in Rancho Santa
Fe, California.[1] They were part of a cult that
had been convinced by their leader, Marshall
Applewhite (who called himself "Do"), that a
spaceship was trailing the comet Hale-Bopp
and it was now prepared to take them to a
higher plane.[2]

But not all were thoroughly convinced.
The group had videotaped last messages to
explain their actions. Looking into the cam-
era one woman with short, cropped hair said,
"Maybe they're crazy for all I know, but I don't
have any choice but to go for it because I've
been on this planet for thirty-one years and
there is nothing here for me."[3] Hers was clearly
not a self-inspired or self-guided death.

Suicide at the request of others

In 1978, in the tragedy of Jonestown, more
than nine hundred people were asked to kill
themselves. Though some were murdered, the
vast majority apparently complied with the
request.[4]

Individual suicides

But it is not just mass suicides like
Heaven's Gate and Jonestown that show us the
power of persuasion. Much more subtle and
pervasive messages have been responsible for
instigating individual suicides. In many individual suicides there are social circumstances
that have combined to convince individuals
they are acting alone and arriving at their own
conclusions, when in fact the depression, desire for death, and even the method employed

are all the result of outside influences.

These outside influences do not necessarily spring from intentional manipulation as was the case in Jonestown and Heaven's Gate. Often social circumstances, and the "modeling" of suicide are enough to create a "suicide cluster," or as it is better known, the "copycat" effect.

Suicide copycats and clusters

It is widely known that Ernest Hemingway took his life with a firearm when he was sixty-two. It is less widely-known that Hemingway had copied his father who had committed suicide in a similar fashion.

While copycat suicides may be found in family groups, these are by no means the only examples of social circumstances influencing a suicidal act. Loren Coleman, in his book *Suicide Clusters*, explores the myriad of social influences from music and movies, to friends and families, that can have a documentable impact on whether or not an individual "chooses" death.[5]

Our social world influences our decisions, even suicidal decisions

Although teen suicide clusters are perhaps the most reported, the cluster effect has also occured in other groups. Families as well as certain social groups and professions (most notably law enforcement), have been susceptible to the copy-cat effect. At present, elderly white men seem to be at great risk. [6]

The clear message of suicide clusters is that exposure to suicide, and acceptance of it, even grudging acceptance (justifying it because of "difficult circumstances") breeds more suicides, and has at times led to a rash of self-murders.

Suicide clusters in history

"Suicide cluster" is a term that has come into usage in recent years, but it is not a new phenomenon. Throughout history and across cultures, family and peers have influenced not only how we dress, and how we live, but sometimes even how we die.

In the writings of the Greek historian Plutarch we find the story of the maidens of Miletus, who followed one another in suicide. The only thing that stopped the epidemic was making it "unfashionable."

Ancient Greece

> A strange and terrible affliction came upon the maidens of Milethos, from some obscure cause... for there fell suddenly upon them a desire for death and a mad impulse towards hanging. Many hanged themselves before they could be prevented.... The plague seemed to be of an unearthly character and beyond human remedy, until on the motion of a wise man a resolution was proposed that women who hanged themselves should be carried out to burial through the market-place. The ratification of this motion not only checked the evil but altogether put an end to the passion for death. A great evidence of the high character and virtue of the women was the shrinking from dishonor and the fact that they were fearless in the face of the two most awful things in the world – death and pain – could not support the appearance of disgrace nor bear the thought of shame after death.[7]

Later Plutarch notes that the decree required the virgins to be carried naked through
the market-place. "The passage of this law not

Public
shame
discouraged
suicide

only inhibited but quashed their desire of killing themselves." The element of "shame after
death," and the public condemnation of suicide appears throughout history as the best
social guardian against repeated individual
acts of self-destruction. Conversely, an empathy for the circumstances of a suicide, even for
just "certain circumstances" is often seen by
potential copy cats as justification, and breeds
an increase in the act, and a broadening of
the circumstances.

The Mihara cluster

Mount Mihara is a volcanic mountain on
the island of Oshima, Japan. In January of
1933, two students jumped into the fiery pit,
convinced that the lava would cremate them
and the smoke transport them to heaven. Reporters became very interested in the story, and

Suicide
tourism

several repeat suicides followed. There were
more news stories, and overnight Oshima became a national attraction. Tourism to the tiny
island increased dramatically. Crowds were
now coming to see the suicides rather than the
volcano. New ferry boats were constructed to
bring the crowds to view the site.

Record has it that on one occasion a man
dared someone from the crowd of tourists to
jump and somebody did! On the first Sunday
of April 1933, six persons took the plunge to
end it all while twenty-five others were prevented by the use of physical force. By the end

of 1933 Mihara had claimed 143 lives.

By 1934, police had noted that they had forcibly prevented 1200 such deaths. An anti-suicide league was formed, yet 619 persons still jumped to their own deaths in 1936. Eventually guards and a high barbed-wire fence helped to put an end to the morbid epidemic.

Commenting on this and the diversity of suicide clusters, Howard Rosenthal says in his book, *Preventing Your Suicide and That of Others,*

Suicide is contagious

> Suicide, seemingly is contagious. If you have one suicide in a school, business, prison, or even in a volcano, the odds increase that you will have others. When a person who is unhappy sees another flee the pain of everyday life via suicide, the person seems now to have permission to do so himself or herself. And though the second, third, or hundredth person to take his or her own life does not always know the other persons who killed themselves, he or she knows of them.[8]

And pointedly he says,

> Not only does one suicide increase the chances that another will occur, but it ups the ante that subsequent acts of self-destruction will be enacted in exactly the same fashion as the initial incident.[9]

Dealing with modern "teen" suicide clusters

It is not untypical in a modern setting for authorities to attempt to stop a "suicide cluster" in exactly the wrong way. After a teen's suicide, for example, a school's principal may gather the student body to explain and hopefully forestall imitators. "I have bad news. Jimmy committed suicide last night," he announces. After the stunned listeners take their breath they now listen, riveted to every word. "We loved Jimmy, but you need to know that he was suffering some emotional problems. His folks had split up. I understand his grades were way down and he had been on drugs. If you feel emotional pressure in any of these areas be sure to see me or a counselor." This last advice is good, but unfortunately the principal has also just re-iterated the "reasons" for Jimmy's suicide. The local news services will likely do the same, running the story and likely adding details on the specific method used.[10]

Giving "reasons" for suicide

Unfortunately in the mind of susceptible individuals the circumstances of Jimmy's life will be compared to the circumstances in their own, and in the case of copycats, parallels will be seen. "My folks have been fighting. I've dabbled in drugs. My grades are shot too. And I sure feel bummed."

Suicide clusters are most effectively quelled where there is immediate intervention, active listening, and availability of trained counselors, but most importantly, there must be a clear and unequivocal condemnation of the act. Such unequivocal judgments are not popular within the "mealy-mouthed," feel-good psychology of our day, but it must be so and the condemnation must be from a social group or individual the potential copycat esteems.

Stopping suicides by condemning the act

Just such effective intervention came into play after the death of Kurt Cobain the popular "grunge" rock star, and considered by some

the figurehead of an entire generation of dis-
affected youth. Tens of thousands of his fans
gathered at the funeral in Seattle; hundreds
of thousands of others would hear the words
spoken that day. Cobain's widow, Courtney
Love, came to the microphone and after speaking briefly of her love for Kurt, surprised every listener when she forcefully concluded,
"What Kurt did was wrong. It accomplished
nothing. It hurt me. It hurt our daughter. And
it hurt all of you. I want you to join me as I
speak to Kurt and say, 'I love you Kurt, but
f*** you Kurt!" The grieving wife again and
again led the assembled fans in what was the
clearest condemnation of the act that subcul-
ture could offer. The entire throng repeatedly
shouted, "F*** you, Kurt!"

Courtney Love clearly condemned suicide

It may have been unorthodox, but it is
clear that on that day, Courtney Love saved
lives.

In early Christianity

Clustering of suicides appears to be directly related to how a culture or sub-culture
reacts to an individual act of self-destruction.
Often groups that tolerated suicide, or did not
directly condemn it, found it became so routine as to be faddish. The actions of an early
Christian sect, the Circumcelliones of North
Africa, had reached this stage by the third century, a.d. Christianity had recognized martyrdom as a definitive sign of sainthood. The
Circumcilliones were a group to whom heaven
was so desirable, and martyrdom so attractive,
that every opportunity to die a martyr was

Justification of suicide encourages copycat behavior

sought, and if not found, the opportunity was created. They sought death and its supposed "automatic sainthood" so flippantly that jumping from cliffs and bridges became common.

To us, "martyrdom" now seems an inappropriate term when the "victim" and the "executioner" are the same person. But at that time it took the intervention of Augustine, the bishop of Hippo, to clearly spell out such actions as heretical. Only with this unequivical statement from an "opinion molder" did the practice stop.

In the Circumcilliones, in the young women of Miletus, and in many contemporary suicide clusters, the justification or acceptance of suicide amongst one's peers is a dominant factor in viewing it as an acceptable act for one's self. On the other side of the coin, we also see that society's holding of suicide in disdain has been its most effective deterrent.

Condemning suicide is the most effective deterrent

Goethe's WERTHER

The Werther effect

Modern Europe saw a wave of suicides in the 1770's after the publication of Goethe's first truly-famous work, *The Sorrows of Young Werther*. The book tells the story of a sensitive and uncompromising youth who commits suicide because of his inability to understand his own passions. The book's popularity brought it to all the college towns of the continent. An epidemic of suicides followed, with victims almost exclusively being the young, educated "peers" of Young Werther.

As the popularity of the book spread – and

with it, suicides – authorities took action. The governments of Germany, Denmark, and Italy banned the book. Officials in Milan purchased all existing copies and destroyed them. The city of Copenhagen prohibited its publication.

In Goethe's time, as well as in antiquity, it is clear that exposure to, and acceptance of suicide bred more suicides. It was only when there was intervention and clear social disdain for the act that the vulnerable did not seek it in any numbers.

"When a person who is unhappy sees another flee the pain of everyday life via suicide, the person seems now to have permission to do so himself or herself."
–Howard Rosenthal

Modern acceptance of assisted suicide

Now, more than two hundred years later, a non-fiction suicide book has been published and sent throughout the "educated" world. *Final Exit*, by Derek Humphry, is a collection of tragic stories with a multitude of suicide recipes employed to "solve" them. The book is subtitled "The Practicalities of Self-Deliverance and Assisted Suicide for the Dying." By 1992 it reached number one position on the *New York Times'* Best Seller List. Humphry claims distribution of more than 500,000 copies.

Suicide propaganda

It is interesting to note that of all the many

diverse methods of death outlined in the book, simultaneous ingestion of alcohol and barbiturates, accompanied by asphyxiation with a plastic bag, is described by Humphry as by far the preferred method of suicide, and his personal favorite.

Plastic bag and overdose

As the "suffocating" sensation might cause an individual distress and panic, Humphry suggests that you overcome the natural fear of suffocation and play around with it until you're comfortable. "Why not have a trial run?" he says. In the book he quotes a fellow suicide aficionado,

"Get comfortable" with suicide method – Derek Humphry

> I was so impressed with the experiment [with the plastic bag] that I performed it for our Hemlock Chapter meeting a week or so later. Everyone was both amused and impressed. I urged them to go home and try it on for themselves in order to get more comfortable with the whole concept.[11]

Not nearly as amusing is the actual effect on others. A study published in *The New England Journal of Medicine* found

Propaganda creates suicides

***Final Exit* copycats**

> The number of suicides by asphyxiation in 1991, the year of publication [of *Final Exit*], and 1992 was twice as high, on average, as the annual numbers in 1984 through 1990. *Final Exit* was found at the scene of nine of the thirty-three suicides by asphyxiation in the year after publication. From the evidence gathered at the death scenes, at least fifteen of the 144 people who committed suicide by asphyxiation or poisoning had probably been exposed to the book. Among the fifteen people who had probably consulted the book, six had no known history of serious

medical illness or evidence of disease at autopsy. Of the fifteen, at least five had a psychiatric history that included a previous suicide attempt, hospitalization, or treatment.[12]

These people had certainly been persuaded to end their life, when it is clear that they need not have done so. Many had no physical illness whatsoever.

This study shows the persuasive effect of *Final Exit* in only one city! How many of the victims had been influenced by the book and simply left no evidence? How many had been influenced by some other aspect of the euthanasia movement? How many would be alive today if counseling and care were offered, instead of an "heroic" view of suicide, and the supposed "bravery" of dispatching those who can't bring themselves to do it?

But who helped them?

While *Final Exit* has certainly had an impact on lone suicides, a frightening consideration is that the purpose of the book is not to promote an individual's taking of their own life, but to promote the implementation of "assisted suicide." It provides clear guidelines on how one individual could "assist" in taking the life of a willing participant, and then skillfully avoid detection and prosecution. When properly followed, participants are instructed to leave no evidence that an "assisted suicide" has taken place. We may never know who was involved in those needless killings. We can never know if there were other motives.

Final Exit implicated in numerous questionable deaths

"Assist" in killing and avoid detection

A guide to murder and its cover-up?

The St. Louis Post-Dispatch reported in November of 1997 that a 38 year-old St. Louis man with a history of depression took his own life. *Final Exit* was among his reading materials. Investigators,

> have documented 11 such cases in five years, where the book ... or copies of its pages were near the body.[13]

"The Right to Die credo [is:] share the dying experience."
– Derek Humphry,
FINAL EXIT

Love conquers fear

Terry Mayo Sullivan also read *Final Exit*. She had asked her husband Kerry to buy it for her after five years of living with amyotrophic lateral sclerosis, (ALS) also known as Lou Gehrig's disease. One day in 1992 after reading a particularly poignant story of physical and emotional suffering as described by Humphry, she decided to follow his recommendation and take the compellingly described final cure. But her husband refused to accommodate such wishes. He redoubled his efforts to help and comfort her, and after much effort designed and implemented a computer device that allowed her to communicate. It changed everything.

Final Exit brings her close to the edge

In 1994 she wrote her story for *Ladies' Home Journal*. The seductive voice of death had been silenced, and the underlying cry for help had been heard,

> I don't think about suicide anymore. My life has meaning again, and I plan to live it fully in the time I have remaining. Most of all, I have so many words of love and thanks to say to my wonderful husband, who never gave up, and never stopped loving me.[14]

Also in 1994, Wesley Smith wrote of a friend, Frances, who, though not terminally ill, decided to kill herself. He and other friends would talk her out of it, then months later, for no apparant reason, she would again announce her suicide wish.

Suicidal evangelism

I had come to believe that she had a whisperer quietly urging her on. After her death, I learned there was indeed such a "voice." I discovered it among her possessions that her executor sent me. Frances had a suicide file (ever the organizer, she kept a file for everything), filled with publications from the Hemlock Society and other writings extolling the moral corrections of self-termination and euthanasia. That these writings had a major influence on Frances there can be no doubt. They were carefully clipped and highlighted in yellow marking ink. Many were dogeared from frequent reading.

"I felt chills run up my spine. It was as if I was reading an exact description of Frances's suicide, so closely had she followed the instructions."

One of the articles was a "how to" piece that told the reader the best drug to take and the proper use of a plastic bag placed over the head to make sure death was not foiled. As I read the piece, I felt chills run up my spine. It was as if I were reading an exact description of Frances's suicide, so closely had she followed the instructions. I also found several articles recounting stories of "good" suicides. These tales, eerily comparable to the religious practice of "witnessing" to spread the faith, had a consistent theme: that suicide could be empowering, beneficial and a positive, even uplifting, experience.[15]

Group effort

Is it merely coincidental that the mass suicides of the Heaven's Gate cult in 1997 also employed the same unique barbiturate, alcohol and plastic bag method of asphyxiation as that outlined by Humphry and the Hemlock society? It was a form of suicide rarely if ever seen before Humphry's description, en-

> *"Not only does one suicide increase the chances that another will occur, but it ups the ante that subsequent acts of self-destruction will be enacted in exactly the same fashion as the initial incident."*
> *— Howard Rosenthal*

dorsement, and promotion. And, while the Heaven's Gate cultists had some wierd, cosmic ideas, it should not be forgotten that, these may have been mixed with other, more mundane and typical motives. The leader and decision maker, Marshall Applewhite, believed himself to be dying of cancer.[16]

Manipulated suicide

Amazingly, advocates of "rational suicide" themselves admit the clear and present danger of manipulated suicide. Margaret Pabst-Battin, a "suicidologist" and Assistant Professor of Philosophy at the University of Utah, is the author of many articles, including the book, *Suicide*. She writes that the notion of rational suicide, one which she accepts, and legality she anticipates,

> gives rise to the possibility of large-scale manipulation of suicide, and the maneuvering of people to choosing suicide when they would not otherwise have done so. This is the other, darker side of the future coin.[17]

Although she is an advocate of "rational suicide" she admits to the strong possibility that relatives or others could subtly push an individual into "choosing" death.

Family pressure

One form of manipulation can occur, says Battin, when a manipulator alters "his victim's immediate and/or long range circumstances in such a way that the victim himself chooses death as preferable to continued life." One form of manipulation could be glaring - like torture. This, of course, would be a form of murder. But, she says,

> much more frequent, however, is the small, not very visible, often even inadvertent kind of manipulation that occurs in domestic situations, where what the manipulator does is to "arrange things" so that suicide becomes – given the other alternatives – the reasonable, even attractive choice for his victim.[18]

Battin goes on to point out that the manipulator does not necessarily have to be conscious of the manipulation for it to take place.

Subtle, even unconscious manipulation

Social pressure

Battin admits an entire society could also be manipulated into changing its values regarding who should live or who should die, once "rational suicide" is accepted. Then society could tacitly project who *should* commit suicide – for their own perceived good and everyone else's.

Society will suggest who should "choose" to die

> The motivation for such manipulation and engineering, in a society confronted with scarcities and fearful of an increasingly large "nonproductive" population, may be very strong. Old age, insanity, poverty, and criminality have also been regarded as grounds for rational suicide in the past; given a society afraid of demands from increasingly large geriatric, ghetto, and institutional populations, we can see how interest in producing circumstantial and ideological changes, in order to encourage such people to choose the "reasonable" way out, might be very strong.[19]

As stated earlier, Dr. Pabst-Battin admits to all these dangers, and is still an advocate of accepting "rational suicides." She ends her essay,

> I myself believe that on moral grounds we must accept, not reject, the notion of rational suicide. But I think we must do so with the clear-sighted view of the moral quicksand into which this notion threatens to lead us; perhaps then we may discover a path around.[20]

Perhaps? We *may* discover a path?! If even a leading suicide advocate tells us that acceptance of suicide in certain, "hard cases" will likely lead to a dangerous "moral quicksand," for the rest of society, it seems so much wiser to avoid such deadly quicksand altogether.

Imminent danger for the vulnerable

There are hundreds of thousands of easily manipulated elderly, incapacitated, and infirm throughout the US, and worldwide millions more. These individuals are in immediate and pressing danger - not only from assisted suicide advocates, but from a calloused and manipulative society that may tire of caring for them.

There are many dignity affirming solutions for the few "hard cases." What is clear however, is that if we consider killing them a way of offering dignity, it will become very difficult, if not impossible to distinguish between "assisted suicide" and "manipulated suicide."

NOTES

1 The observations of Nick Matzorkis who was familiar with the cult and discovered the bodies. Quoted in *USA Today*, March 27, 1997, p.1.

2 There is an important footnote to this tragic story that is directly related to Hemlock Society philosophy and indicates the strong possibility of a link between the two separate entities. One of the apparent catalysts for Applewhite's tragic decision was his mistaken impression that he was dying of cancer; Heaven's Gate would be without their leader.The method of death employed by all was an exact reenactment of Humphry's unusual, but preferred method of self-deliverance as outlined in *Final Exit*.

3 *USA Today*, March 27, 1997, p. 1

4 Ibid..

5 Loren Coleman, *Suicide Clusters* (Winchester, MA: Faber and Faber, 1987).

6 Men account for 80% of the suicides in the U.S. The highest rate of suicide is amongst elderly white men over the age of 65, with a rate of 42.7 per 100,000. *Suicide and Life Threatening Behavior*, Volume 25, Number 1, Spring, 1995.

7 Plutarch, *Morals*, and quoted in Coleman.

8 Howard Rosenthal, *Not With My Life You Don't: Preventing Your Suicide and That of Others* (Muncie, IN: Accelerated Development Publishers, 1988), p. 97.

9 Rosenthal, p. 100.

10 Mental Health Administration's *Report of the Secretary's Task Force on Youth Suicide*, vol. 2; "Mass Media and Youth Suicide Prevention" by Alan L. Berman, Washington D.C. 1989.

11 Humphry, *Final Exit*, p.99

12 Marzuk, Peter M., "Increase in Suicide by Asphyxiation in New York City After the Publication of *Final Exit*," 329 *New England Journal of Medicine* 1508 (1993).

13 "Investigators Link Suicide Book to 11 Local Deaths," St. Louis Post-Dispatch, 11/16/97. B1.

14 "A Woman Today: The Language of Love," *Ladies' Home Journal*, March 1994, p. 28.

15 Smith, Wesley J. "The Whispers of Strangers." *National Right to Life News*, Feb. 3, 1994. Originally appeared in *Newsweek*.

16 *USA Today*, 3/27/97. p.1. Although Applewite believed himself to be dying of cancer, thus leaving the obsequiously obedient followers without a leader, the subsequent autopsy showed that he was mistaken. There was no cancer present.

17 M.Pabst-Battin, *Suicide* (New York: Prentice-Hall, 1987). p. 170.

18 Ibid., p. 171.

19 Ibid.

20 Ibid.

CHAPTER TEN

PROMOTIONAL CONSIDERATION
HOW OUR MINDS HAVE BEEN CHANGED
- ASSISTED SUICIDE, MASS COMMUNICATIONS, AND PUBLIC OPINION

In 1989, Dr. Jack Kevorkian was an unknown pathologist, a gaunt and solitary man with a quirky fixation on death. He was "unknown" that is, until he appeared with his suicide machine on the Geraldo show.[1] The rest is history. Janet Adkins, a Portland, Oregon woman who had recently been diagnosed with Alzheimer's ended her life in the back of his Volkswagen van. The sodium pentothal and potassium chloride administered through his simple device had quickly stilled her life.

Mrs. Adkins was, even by Hemlock definitions, nowhere near terminal. (Their *Death with Dignity Act* suggests a prognosis of six months.) In fact, the tape made by Kevorkian before her death, and shown on PBS, shows her to be quite lucid and active. She had even played a tennis match with her son the day before, and won! Death and even severe symptoms of debilitation due to Alzheimer's would still be years in the future under normal circumstances. What would prompt an apparently intelligent woman to such an act? Try television and the power of suggestion for starters.

Advertising

The influence we as individuals feel from others is inescapable and undeniable. Even the mere opinion of others, whether real or perceived, is enough to prompt us to do things that wouldn't otherwise occur to us. This "power of suggestion" is what sells cars, clothes, and toothpaste. It is the necessary catalyst of a consumer culture; it is our plainest evidence that the values and actions of individuals can be altered on a mass scale. As Eric Clark the author of *The Want Makers: Inside the World of Advertising*, put it,

Power of mass communication

> Advertising is far from impotent and harmless: it is not a mere mirror image. Its power is real, and on the brink of a great increase. Not the power to brainwash overnight, but the power to create subtle and real change. The power to prevail.[2]

Sociologist Ronal Berman is more to the point,

> In the absence of traditional authority, ad-

vertising has become a kind of social guide. It depicts us in all the myriad situations possible to a life of free choice. It provides ideas about style, morality, behavior[3]

Public opinion

Public opinion polls have shown a steady increase in social acceptance of "assisted suicide" and other forms of euthanasia. There have no doubt been many reasons for this. But one of the most dramatic factors is glaringly obvious. No functional member of modern society can have escaped what has been an unabashedly concerted attempt to "market" assisted suicide to our culture.

Derek Humphry, the principal co-founder of the Hemlock Society was propelled to fame after his involvement in the death of his first wife, Jean. Few realized at the time that much of that fame had been self-engineered, and that Humphry was a master, a self-described "advocacy journalist," who had been a member of the trade for thirty-five years.[3] Humphry used every trick to promote both himself and his message. And the media, particularly the American media, willingly complied.

Advocacy journalism

Making the news

In fact, not only did the American media culture accommodate Humphry and his message, he found vocal adherents within its ranks. Betty Rollin, a correspondent for NBC for nine years before joining ABC News, implemented the Hemlock creed and facilitated her mother's death. She, like Humphry, then wrote a book, *Last Wish*, and, using her skill as a communicator and her media contacts, she went on the circuit. Every major media market – in addition to the national outlets – heard from Rollin as well as Humphry.[4] Parallel stories and vignettes on "suffering" and the "hopelessly terminal" accompanied the promotion of the books. The "echo effect," where one medium draws from another, gave a repetitive voice to the euthanasia message.[5]

Media echo

Give them what they want

There were other factors that fed the media frenzy, aside from the experienced advocacy found in Humphry, Rollin, and the other media savvy euthanasia advocates. It was a good story. In order to attract viewers and readers, modern reporting has moved away from the balanced give and take analysis once assumed to be present in all good reporting, and embraced a dramatic or titillating sensationalism. In order to have a "good story," there must be conflict, and there must be something of unusual interest. (The anxious editor's maxim is, "'Dog Bites Man' is not a story; 'Man Bites Dog' *is*.") Assisting a suicide, and boldly and bravely breaking the law to do it, certainly fit the sensational model.

A good story

But there is one other element in "mercy killing" that attracted both reporters and editors, as well as producers and directors – emotion. And as psychologists are well aware, the emotions surrounding death and dying are universally shared. Everyone has deep-seated

Emotion

feelings about this issue.

"Helping the suffering to die" was a dream story handed to the average reporter on a platter. Any detailed analysis or critique would throw a wet blanket over its "immediate appeal." In short, this was a story that was good for the market, and by all means they would market it. Having advocates who were accomplished, knowledgeable, and experienced in both euthanasia *and the media* only made a producer's job easier.

Publicity Obsession Pays Off For Suicide-Book Publisher

By F⸱ ⸱ ⸱ COHEN   pub'   ⸱⸱id
                        r

NEW YORK TIMES
August 26, 1991

The promoters of **Final Exit**
went to extraordinary lengths.

The news affects our minds

The role of the mass media in the growing acceptability of suicide is a demonstrated fact. The research shows – and this is what is perhaps most ominous – that media coverage has affected not just the acceptance of suicide and assisted suicide, but the fulfillment of the act.

In the 1980's David Phillips researched

and published detailed analyses of U.S. teen suicides between 1973-79. He found a direct and alarming correlation between placement of newspaper stories and subsequent suicides. The more prominent the story, the greater the number of copycat suicides. In 1986 the *New England Journal of Medicine* published another of his studies, reporting an even greater increase after television news stories about suicide.[6]

Newspaper stories contribute to suicide

In 1989, the Center for Disease Control convened a national workshop which confirmed that certain forms of news reporting were direct contributors to suicide contagion. Due to First Amendment concerns about "censorship," no definitive regulations were devised. "General concerns and recommendations" were posited, but publication of those was delayed until 1994.[7]

Not just the news

Phillips' 1982 study was the the first of its kind to clearly and systematically show evidence of the direct correlation between fictional television suicides and real "copycats."[8]

In 1986 British researchers found that Phillips' observations about soap opera suicides rang true in that country as well. In the week following March 2, 1986, when the popular BBC program *The Easterners* depicted a suicide attempt, suicide attempts throughout England increased remarkably. Some hospitals reported triple the incidence of overdose attempts (the method depicted). Some hospitals even ran out of beds! Doctors Simon Ellis

Broadcasts of fictional accounts contribute to copycats

and Susan Walsh wrote in the medical journal *The Lancet,*

> Do the BBC programmers consider the likely consequences of screening self-destructive behavior that is likely to be copied? Next time, could they please arrange for Angie to take an overdose in the summer when our bed state is not so acute?[9]

Other studies have documented the sharp jump in the number of "Russian roulette" suicides after the TV showing or video rental use of the movie *The Deer Hunter,* which depicts such a suicide. Even dramatic programming ostensibly designed to "prevent" suicides have been shown to contribute to them.[10]

It is not just the "lone" suicide, but, sadly, assisted suicide has also had its share of promotional consideration in the dramatic arts. Richard Dreyfus portrayed a disabled artist seeking help in suicide in the 1981 film, *Whose Life Is It Anyway?* Disability rights activists protested the depiction of his condition as false and demeaning. Care to take a stab at how it ends? Other made-for-televsion movies dramatised real scenarios, in some cases lionizing those who had committed illegal "mercy killing."

One such show was *The Roswell Gilbert Story*. The program, which aired early in 1987, stars the actor Robert Young, whose public persona of benign, paternal good judgement was known to millions of Americans through his title roles in *Father Knows Best,* and *Marcus Welby M.D.*. Young portrayed Roswell Gilbert, an elderly Floridian who only months earlier was convicted in the shooting death of his se-

Suicide contagion spurred by programming

Whose Life Is It Anyway?

nile wife. The movie was instrumental in win-
ning the release of the real Gilbert.

To recognize the continued Hollywood
embrace of euthanasia chic, one need look no
further than the runaway Academy Award win-
ner for 1997, *The English Patient*. The film
lovingly depicts an assisted suicide as a poignant and touching end to a star-crossed "ro-

Hollywood mance."
makes its
mark   There is overwhelming evidence that the
popular media has a direct and dramatic effect on viewers' opinions, values, and actions.
Despite this, individuals in the performing
arts, and Hollywood in particular, tend to
downplay the deadly influence they can have
on individuals. However, they will acknowledge
their influence when they are praised.

In accepting the Humanitas Award for
Dead Man Walking in 1997, actor and director Tim Robbins unequivically claimed for
himself successful manipulation of the culture,
"You really can effect change through television and movies."[11]

Polls

If individuals can be convinced to kill
themselves through outside factors, like news
and the movies, should we be surprised if one's
opinions are not also affected? In the last
twenty years Americans seem to have grown
accustomed to assisted suicide (they are after
all good media consumers); but this is not a
wholesale endorsement, as some polls would
suggest. As in most opinion polls, one of the
principal factors in the outcome is making sure
the respondent understands the real issue, and
the nature of the question itself.

When a person has a disease that cannot be cured, do you think doctors should be allowed to end the patient's life by some painless means if the patient and his family request it?

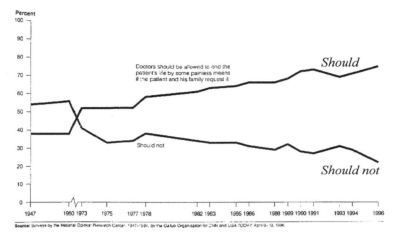

Source: Surveys by the National Opinion Research Center, 1947-1994, by the Gallup Organization for CNN and USA TODAY, April 9- 10, 1996.

Pollsters began asking Americans about assisted suicide fifty years ago, though the question does not make the distinction between forgoing life-sustaining treatment and actively providing drugs to end life. In 1947, majorities opposed assisted suicide; today, strong majorities support it. Majorities apparently believe suicide is acceptable when a person has an incurable disease.[12]

Other polls

While some polls indicate broad support for assisted suicide, others show hesitation, particularly by those who would be most affected: the elderly and the poor.

A poll conducted for the *Washington Post* on March 22-26, 1996 found 50% support for legalizing physician-assisted suicide. Voters aged 35-44 supported legislation, 57% to 33%. But these figures were reversed for voters aged 65 and older, who opposed such legislation

54% to 38%. Majority opposition was also
found among those with incomes under
$15,000 (54%) and black Americans (70%).[13]

Public opinion has clearly changed over
the years. Many in our society are apparently
now willing to embrace assisted suicide. But
the changes in opinion have not been the result of serious analysis, and those most at risk
have strong reservations about what this
means for them.

<u>NOTES</u>

1 But was Janet also manipulated? There is a chilling version of the Janet
  Adkins story retold in Kevorkian's book, *Prescription: Medicide* (Buf-
  falo, NY: Prometheus Books, 1991) p. 221. Months before the television program seen by Janet aired, Kevorkian says he received a call
  from a Ron Adkins,

> who learned of my campaign from an item in *Newsweek* (No
> vember 13, 1989). He calmly explained the tragic situation of
> his beloved wife ... who, for some time, had noticed gradually
> progresive impairment of her memory. [She had learned of]
> the diagnosis of Alzheimer's disease four months earlier.

  As in many such cases, the individual who would likely be the
  primary care-giver, instead of offering hope and encouragement, be-
  comes the primary facilitator of suicide.

2 Eric Clark, *The Want Makers: Inside the World of Advertising* (New York:
  Penguin Books, 1988), p. 20.

3 Ronald Berman, *Advertising and Social Change*, (Beverly Hills, CA: Sage Press, 1981), p. 13.

4 Humphry worked for the *Sunday Times* of London, and was particularly proud of his unabashed advocacy of social issues. (In "advocacy journalist" *advocacy* is used as an adjective to make the clear distinction between this form of journalism and *reporting*.) When he came to the United States in the early '80's he worked for the *Los Angeles Times*, despite his involvement as full-time leader of the Hemlock Society.

In addition to ABC and NBC, Rollin has been an editor and writer at *Vogue* and *Look*, and has written for the *New York Times* and *McCall's*.

5 It is a common practice for broadcast journalists to draw their stories from print, and for features to be assigned to coincide with "top stories."

6 David Phillips and Lundie Christensen, in the *New England Journal of Medicine*, September, 1986, cited in Coleman, p. 96 (see chapter 9 footnote 5).

7 Center for Disease Control website. "Suicide Contagion and the Reporting of Suicide: Recommendations from a National Workshop." [http://aepo-xdv-www.epo.cdc.gov/wonder/prevguid/m0031539/entire/htm], June 1, 1997.

8 Coleman, pg. 97.

9 Ibid.

10 The February 10, 1985 showing of the ABC-TV made-for-television movie *Surviving* starring Zach Galligan and Molly Ringwald was linked to numerous suicides. Coleman (pg. 100) cites studies by Madelyn Gould and David Shaffer of Columbia University which shows an alarming jump in suicides following four such t.v. movies broadcast between October 1984 and February 1985.

11 "Hollywood: Religion Gains Acceptance." *Los Angeles Times*, April 1, 1997, p. A16.

12 "Physician-assisted Suicide." *The American Enterprise*, January/February 1997, p. 91.

13 *Washington Post*, April 4, 1996, p. A18

CHAPTER
ELEVEN
ADVANCE DIRECTIVES

Advance directives are an important part of the debate about end-of-life issues. Euthanasia advocates have sought to legalize assisted suicide by amending existing living-will laws and creating a new form of advance medical directive.[1]

Advance directives are legal documents which indicate an individual's desires for treatment should he or she become incapacitated. There are two basic types of advance directive - living wills, which specify the extent and nature of treatment, and Durable Powers of Attorney for Health Care, which essentially empower another, specific individual to make decisions for the incapacitated.

The problem with living wills

It is pleasant to think that should we ever be incapacitated and unable to communicate our wishes, a legal document would go into effect that would allow our "will" to continue to direct our lives. While that is often the intent of the "living will" it is not necessarily the result. In fact the use of the living will has created some serious problems in the treatment of vulnerable individuals and in the doctor-patient relationship.

The chess game

To better understand the drawbacks of the living will, imagine you had the opportunity to play in a world-class chess tournament. Since you lose even at checkers, to make up for your ignorance of the game you are allowed to delegate all of your decisions to chess champion Bobby Fisher. What a pleasure to watch him brilliantly overcome your adversaries, and all in your name! Then before the final game begins you slip him an envelope with these instructions, "If you are ever put in check, you are to surrender the game." Fisher would be aghast, for being put in check is not an uncommon event in a chess game.

In much the same way, being in danger of one's life is not uncommon to the practice of medicine, but the living will essentially functions much as your note to the chessmaster would. Because of this, the living will has dramatically chilled the practice of life-saving, interventive medicine.

Unnecessary

It is often
hard to
know if a
patient is
dying

It is, and has been, ethically acceptable for doctors to withdraw extraordinary medical procedures from dying patients and to withhold truly futile treatment. But a legally-binding living will places doctors in a difficult situation. Decisions as to what are or are not unreasonable treatment often depend on the circumstances of each unique case. When the living will is legally binding and if it prohibits interventive care, the special individual and personal care necessary in such delicate circumstances is lost.

Bias for death

The living will carries with it a strong bias toward non-treatment and death. It is often extremely difficult to determine when a patient's illness is terminal. When there is some question about the provisions or enforcement of a living will, physicians often feel pressured to simply not treat the patient at all, for risk of being sued. (See page 167.) The frequency and high cost of such suits places a tremendous burden on the physician. It is often easier to simply play it safe.

When the question of legal enforcement of living will type documents was debated in Great Britain, the British National Council for Hospice and Palliative Care concluded,

The bias against treatment in some advance directives is so strong as to limit the autonomy of the health care team and informal carers. For instance, some suggested directives dictate that in the event of Alzheimer's disease all life-sustaining treatment should cease. This would forbid the giving of insulin to a diabetic patient with Alzheimer's disease if the directive were legally binding. Withdrawal of insulin in these circumstances might well be morally objectionable to the whole health care team...[2]

Ignoring 'Right to Die' Directives, Medical Community Is Being Sued

By TAMAR LEWIN

...... that they doing what was best could not

NEW YORK TIMES,
June 2, 1996

Is that how you are going to feel then?

The healthy do not make their choices in the same way as the sick. You may not want to live out a hypothetical life in a wheelchair; who would? But if you actually were disabled your perspective on life would be dramatically different.

During the British debate mentioned above, numerous studies were presented that came to the same conclusion; in principle, it is not a good idea to make a specific decision now about a hypothetical event sometime in the future. As a group of Canadian doctors found,

> The authors conclude that: an advance directive prepared by a healthy person is not a valid indicator of the preferences of a similar person when sick....Our experience is that people change their minds when they become unwell, but an earlier advance directive might still be in force.[3]

Delegating to a trusted individual

The second type of advance directive is the Durable Power of Attorney for Healthcare (DPAHC). Instead of simply giving orders for a future, unknown event, the DPAHC delegates the decisionmaking to another individual. Particular wishes can be made known, but the proxy decisionmaker is granted final decision-making authority.

It is important to note that "next of kin," though often encumbered with this authority,

Family may not be the best advocates

do not necessarily make the best decision-makers. With powers of attorney it is often better to appoint individuals who may not be family members, but whose judgement you trust, those who can bring a more studied and less "turmoiled" point of view to the decision.

Problems with family members

James Bopp of the National Legal Center for the Medically Dependent and Disabled points out that there are numerous reasons not to automatically give family members unlimited decisionmaking power for incompetent relatives.[4]

First, the lack of medical information in the family, (much as our inexperienced "chessplayer" would be unwise to take the end game into his own hands). Second, family decisions are often influenced by emotional reactions. Third, family decisions often suffer from an inability to separate interests. Bopp quotes one researcher,

> A reasonable patient would not choose as a proxy someone who is of the opinion that the patient's continued existence constitutes a threat to the decision-maker.[5]

Fourth, family decisions often suffer from the influence of a family's financial interest. Fifth, studies have shown that many family members do not appreciate and underestimate the capabilities, albeit limited, of certain patients that they remember as having been fully functional.

Automatically making the family the decisionmaker places them in a difficult spot. The process can be tormenting, and disagreements about treatment can create intense friction in family relationships. Finally, giving family members ultimate-decision powers may falsely assume a close family bond.

An American problem

The confusion over advance directives was made even greater in 1991 by the Patient's Self-Determination Act. The new federal regula-

Determination Act. The new federal regulations were enacted requiring every hospital, hospice, nursing home and health maintenance organization participating in Medicare or Medicaid to present patients with the right to refuse treatment and sign advance directives. Given the lack of public understanding, this new law has created confusion, and perpetuates greater presumption for non-treatment and simple "health maintenance."

The will to live

A new form of durable power of attorney has been drawn up which doesn't automatically skew a proxy decisionmakers choices toward non-treatment.

Presumption for living

The "Will to Live" is an important addition to the current collection of advance directives, as it seeks to provide a presumption that *the patient would like to live.* This is an unusual idea for some who promote the widespread use of advance directives. It also fulfills the requirements of the Patient's Self-Determination Act, allowing you to appoint a proxy whose judgement you trust, as well as allowing you to make clear to them what medical treatment you would want if you can no longer speak for yourself.

Will to Live forms are available to conform with the laws of the various states. For more information contact: Medical Ethics Project, 419 7th Street NW, Suite 400, Washington, D.C. 20004.

NOTES

1 Robert Risley and Michael White, *The Humane and Dignified Death Act* (Los Angeles: Hemlock Society, 1986).

2 *Proceeding of the House of Lords Select Committee on Medical Ethics,* Vol.II. July 13, 1993, p. 208.

3 M.C. Tierney, et al. "How Reliable are Advance Directives for Healthcare? A study of the attitudes of the healthy and unwell to treatment of the terminally ill." Toronto: The Annals of the Royal College of Physicians and Surgeons of Canada, 1992.

4 James Bopp, Jr., and Richard E. Coleson, "A Critique of Family Members as Proxy Decision Makers Without Legal Limits." *Issues in Law and Medicine*, Vol 12, no. 2. Fall 1996.

5 Norman Fost, "Counseling Families who have a Child with a Severe Congenital Anomaly." 67 *Pediatrics* 321,322. 1981. Quoted in Bopp.

CHAPTER TWELVE

CIVIL DEFENSE AGAINST EUTHANASIA

Prosecuting acts of assisted suicide has proved difficult. Why was Jack Kevorkian still a free man after being implicated in nearly fifty deaths, and after being tried several times? Kevorkian had been tried in criminal court by the Oakland County (Michigan) prosecutor, but to no avail. Each failure to convict the brazen death peddler was worn by him as a badge of honor, invoked by him as justification of his deadly trade. And all of this continued despite clear evidence that many of his "patients" had no terminal illness.

At the same time that Kevorkian was being prosecuted (1995/96) another pair of deaths caught the international spotlight, those of Nicole Brown Simpson and Ron Goldman. The results of those cases serve as a good example as to how society might more effectively deal with assisted suicide perpetrators. Simply put, the O.J. Simpson murder cases reveal certain inadequacies of criminal prosecution, while the subsequent wrongful death suit showed the successful application of civil action.

Learning from O.J.

In the first Simpson trial, he faced criminal prosecution, and Simpson was found "not guilty" despite what many perceived to be overwhelming evidence of his guilt. However, in the following civil trial he was quickly found guilty of wrongful death, and required to pay millions of dollars to the families of those he killed. The reason for the discrepancy is the much higher standard of evidence in American criminal proceedings as opposed to that required for civil trials.

The problem of prosecuting assisted suicide

Because a request for death has long been recognized as an emotional cry for help, and society has historically responded with dramatic interventions to address the emotional despair, the simplistic act of dispatching a despairing individual has been considered a callous and criminal act. Every state in the Union, and most other countries, have treated assisted suicide as a crime.

Standards of evidence

However, the ability to obtain a conviction for such a crime has long been impeded by the evidence requirement for criminal action, the cases of Kevorkian and Simpson may serve as examples. But the standard of evidence is only one barrier to legally stopping the assistance of suicide.

Under the American system of criminal law it is entirely up to the local prosecutor to bring action. This privilege of "prosecutorial discretion" allows the local district attorney to simply not file charges in those cases that may appear futile. In fact records indicate that the successful prosecution of assisted suicide is relatively rare.[1]

An article in the *Columbia Law Review* reports,

> Police and prosecutors appear to be reluctant to bring charges for suicide assistance. A British study found only one-sixth of all reported cases of suicide assistance were prosecuted.... It seems plain that police and prosecutors are exercising their discretion to turn a blind eye to acts of assistance to suicide, which means that legislative enactments are not being enforced.[2]

Local prosecutors may be unwilling to bring action for any number of reasons. First may be political implications; Oakland County Prosecutor Dravic, who unsuccessfully indicted Kevorkian, lost his re-election bid in 1996; Kevorkian supporters had targeted him as an example for other District Attorneys.

But there may be other reasons that so few criminal cases are pursued after an assisted suicide. Often those involved are sympathetic figures, doctors or family members or friends of the victim, and appear to be much more benevolent characters than the common criminal. Retribution against such individuals is often seen as heavy-handed and is rarely successful.

Prosecutors' priorities

Political consideration

As Dr. David O'Steen and attorney Burke Balch comment in an article discussing the prosecutor's challenge,

> If a prosecution does in fact come to trial, and against the odds a conviction is secured, a dilemma occurs. If a stiff jail sentence is given, the defendant may well come to be seen as a martyr; if a lenient one, the deterrent value of the law will be greatly undermined. In either case, respect for the law is diminished, and pressure for its repeal–as either "draconian" or "ineffective"–is likely to grow.[3]

Jailing martyrs

Take 'em to court

As illustrated in the famous Simpson case, private individuals, like the families of Goldman and Brown, are given legal "standing," the right to sue the perpetrator. They are often successful where criminal prosecutors are not.

In the case of assisted suicide, a suicide "assistant" or "implementer" could be sued by the families of the victims. Two types of remedies can be brought in such cases, injunctions and civil damages.

Injunctions are of particular importance in dealing with assisted suicide as they can be used to prevent the act before it happens, which ultimately is the goal of the law.[4] A violation of such a court ordered mandate would result in heavy fines for contempt of court. Such penalties would likely have a more dramatic effect than the improbable jail time imposed under criminal prosecution. As the typi-

Injunctions can save lives

cal physician's generic fear of malpractice suits would seem to indicate, financial sanctions are often an effective deterrent. And financial penalities can be enforced through garnishment of income or seizure of assets.

Civil penalties would discourage doctors from abetting suicide

Civil damages are a second weapon in the armory of civil penalties. These are financial awards granted after the fact, as in a typical malpractice case. Not only are such penalties a daunting prospect for the perpetrator, but insurance companies who would likely be drawn in to pay such suits would put pressure on physicians to avoid activities that may subject them to such fines.

A civil response

While the criminal laws against assisting in the suicide of a vulnerable individual have been effective for hundreds of years, today they are under concerted attack, and are being rendered ineffective. The enactment, pursuit, and enforcement of civil remedies for such cases, as opposed to simple reliance on criminal laws, may be our best chance at restoring protection for the depressed and vulnerable.

Kevorkian still a step ahead

It should be noted that Jack Kevorkian, who is seeking to be prosecuted for notoriety's sake, has insulated himself from harmful litigation. As noted earlier, criminal prosecution is very difficult, and if successful, would make him a jailed martyr. And as he has no personal wealth or property (he lives in a house owned by his attorney) contempt of court charges are the most severe penalty presently available to stop him.

Nevertheless, such civil penalties would go

a long way to ensure that normal physicians would think twice before facilitating the death of a vulnerable patient.

Notes

1 David O'Steen and Burke Balch, "The Need for Civil Remedies to Prevent Assisting Suicide," (Washington D.C: National Right to Life Committee, 1993).

2 *Columbia Law Review* (1986) quoted in O'Steen, "Need for Civil Remedies."

3 O'Steen and Balch.

4 The Gerald Klooster case is just an example of such an injunction. The son of an Alzheimer's patient successfully sued to prevent the patient's wife from arranging a "visit" with Kevorkian.

FREQUENTLY ASKED QUESTIONS

In discussing assisted suicide, or any aspect of death and dying, it is critically important to recognize first the emotional underpinnings that give form to one's fears and biases about death. Dr. Cicely Saunders refers to "total pain," the emotional, psychological, and even sociological pain that surrounds death itself, and the death of a loved one in particular. This "total pain" or emotional predisposition must first be addressed before the facts surrounding assisted suicide can be considered with a clear mind.

Failure to recognize the emotional foundation of assisted suicide's lure will often result in discussing the right issues and providing the right answers with what is essentially an unreceptive audience. It is therefore essential that the emotions of the assisted suicide debate be first recognized, then acknowledged, and then disffused if one is to successfully bring reason to the table.

WHAT IF SOMEONE IS IN INTOLERABLE PAIN?

The fact is that with few exceptions, there is pain control available for even the most difficult of cancers. If you or a loved one is in uncontrolled pain and your physician is not responding to requests for better pain management, then do what any medical professional would do – get another doctor.

See pages 23-43

I DON'T SEE MUCH DIFFERENCE BETWEEN LETTING SOMEONE DIE AND SIMPLY HELPING THEM DIE IN PEACE. WHY CAN'T WE LEGALIZE ASSISTED SUICIDE FOR THOSE SITUATIONS WHERE TECHNOLOGY IS SIMPLY KEEPING THE PATIENT ALIVE? AREN'T YOU FORCING PEOPLE TO STAY ALIVE?

Euthanasia advocates often exploit the confusion of the general public as to what is already legal. There is a world of difference between tending to the needs of an individual on their deathbed and causing their death. The now-common practice of *providing basic comfort care* after extraordinary measures have been withdrawn cannot be equated with killing the same patient. In the first case a patient dies from the effect of their illness; in the other, death comes because the patient has been intentionally killed.

See page 45

See page 96

BUT IF SOMEONE IS REQUESTING SUICIDE, IT IS A PERSONAL DECISION. WHO ARE WE TO DENY THAT?

Suicide attempts and requests for suicide have long been recognized by psychologists as a cry for help. Well-intentioned individuals who support a request for suicide are often reinforcing the feeling that the patient's life has lost all meaning and is now nothing but a burden, when in fact the patient is actually searching for affirmation and encouragement. Competent counseling for family and patient are the appropriate response for those who seek death, not abetting it.

See page 3

See pages 24-25

See pages 129-130

AREN'T WE KINDER TO PUPPY DOGS THAN WE ARE TO PEOPLE? AT LEAST ANIMALS GET HUMANE TREATMENT AND ARE "PUT TO SLEEP."

This is a very common assertion based on a very misguided premise. The fact is that animals are frequently dispatched, not because we, as a society, esteem them as worthy of greater care than humans, but because we value them less.

See page 24

The treatment for rabies, for example, entails considerable cost and trouble, but it is freely expended on a human being in a valiant effort to save that life. On the other hand, it is not unusual to simply destroy a rabies-infected animal.

See page 83

It is commonly known that a mediocre racehorse is often destroyed if it breaks a leg, but veterinarians do not offer this as a useful model for human practice. We treat animals differently than we treat people because they

See pages 95-96

are different.

BUT IF SOMEONE IS TERMINALLY ILL AND REQUESTS SUICIDE, DON'T YOU THINK THEIR LIFE REALLY COULD BE A BURDEN?

Experts like Dr. Elizabeth Kubler-Ross (who quite literally wrote the book, *On Death and Dying*), point out that this is a very common feeling. Kubler-Ross identifies emotional stages that are common to those with a terminal diagnosis: Denial, Anger, Bargaining, Depression and Acceptance, and with acceptance, emotional growth. If the patient and family are properly counseled, Kubler-Ross sees the facing of mortality as a psychological benefit, a truly dynamic "growth experience."

See page 17

"Lots of my dying patients say they grow in bounds and leaps, and finish all the unfinished business," she says. Assisting their suicide is "cheating them of these lessons.... That's not love."

See page 21

Ironically, it is after passing through the suicidal depressive stages and on through the "acceptance" stage that the patient is not only most likely to experience emotional growth, but this emotional maturity also seems to be a factor in many cases of remission. All of these benefits are lost if we agree to suicide on request.

OKAY, BUT IN HOLLAND, EUTHANASIA HAS BEEN LEGALIZED AND PRACTICED SUCCESSFULLY, HASN'T IT?

In fact, a report released by the Dutch government in 1991 reveals that there have been more abuses than the popular media has cared to cover. In 1990 there were 11,800 recorded cases in which the doctor actively caused death. Of these, 5941 were done without the patient's consent. In other words, **more than half of those killed did not ask for it!**

See page 72

In late 1991, the Dutch Parliament introduced "rules of careful conduct," but these still allow doctors to practice active euthanasia without the consent of the patient. Though there are now loose rules on such things, even the leading Dutch specialist in pediatric oncology has admitted to providing poison to children in his care without seeking the parents' consent.

See pages 61-79

In 1994, the Dutch Supreme Court held as justifiable the case of a psychologist who assisted the suicide of a *physically healthy* 50-year old woman who was merely depressed! She had no underlying physical illness, but was depressed over personal losses. What was the doctor's treatment for the depression? He decided to abet it, to accommodate her suicidal thoughts and facilitate her suicidal actions.

THAT'S HOLLAND. BUT CAN'T WE CAREFULLY CREATE A VERY NARROW LAW HERE THAT ONLY ALLOWS SUCH ACTIONS FOR THE REALLY HARD CASES, WHERE PEOPLE REALLY AND TRULY WANT TO DIE OF THEIR OWN FREE WILL?

Dutch problems aside, our knowledge of suicide itself should warn us away from such a course. Suicide clusters among common social groups have been recognized for centuries and the lessons learned from them will serve us well now. The "cluster" phenomenon is the occurrence of suicide within a peer group, followed by other attempts within the group. They have occurred amongst the young, in groups of a common profession, and amongst the elderly. **These increasingly-common social phenomena demonstrate just how easily even healthy individuals can be convinced that suicide is right for them.** One lesson psychologists have gleaned from dealing with clusters is that the swift condemnation of the act and intervention by competent counselors is the best way to prevent more suicides.

See page 139

WHY IS THE SOCIAL ENVIRONMENT SUCH AN INFLUENCING FACTOR ON A VERY PERSONAL DECISION?

You tell me. It is known that what we think our social peers feel about an action impacts how we will feel about that action. That's what sells toothpaste - and most everything else, for that matter!

See page 17

See pages 154-155

SO YOU THINK ACCEPTING AN ASSISTED SUICIDE LAW WOULD PUT PRESSURE ON PEOPLE TO KILL THEMSELVES, OR SUBTLY CAUSE THEM TO ASK OTHER PEOPLE TO KILL THEM. ISN'T THAT BEING A BIT OF AN ALARMIST? WHY SHOULD I BELIEVE THAT?

Aside from the facts already mentioned, a good reason to be concerned is that even advocates of "rational suicide" admit the very real dangers of accepting a change in the law. Margaret Pabst-Battin is an outspoken advocate of "rational suicide," but even she sees dangers that she is willing to begrudgingly accept. She writes in her essay, "Manipulated Suicide:"

See pages 149-150

> (Rational suicide) gives rise to the possibility of large-scale manipulation of suicide and the maneuvering of persons into choosing suicide when they would not otherwise have done so. This is the other, darker side of the future coin.

As pointed out by the influence of suicide literature on suicides discovered in New York City, this darker possibility is not lurking somewhere out in the future. Never mind legalizing it – the mere promotion of assisted suicide has taken countless lives already.

See pages 144-145

BUT DON'T ADVOCATES OF ASSISTED SUICIDE ONLY WANT IT LEGALIZED FOR THOSE PEOPLE WHO ARE TERMINALLY ILL?

No. Most of Kevorkian's victims were not terminal, but they were debilitated. The non-terminal handicapped and those who are not terminal, but "decrepit," are also considered acceptable candidates by euthanasia advocates.

See page 52-60

WHAT ABOUT THE INCREDIBLE COST OF KEEPING THESE PEOPLE AROUND?

If it is recognized as burdensome or unnecessary, extraordinarily costly care *can already be withdrawn.* As mentioned earlier, the withdrawal of extraordinary treatment is not what euthanasia advocates are trying to attain. Their goal is to shape the law so that it is socially permissible to take lethal measures against an individual. The patient does not then die from an underlying illness; they die because of their treatment.

See page 96

When it comes to actual cost, the basic comfort care required for the elderly and disabled is, in fact, minimal in expense. *The cost of emotional care and personal involvement is what is often the motivating factor in family abandonment in these cases.* But there are resources and alternatives available for difficult situations; killing the family member should not be one of them.

See pages 121-123

WITH ADVANCES IN TECHNOLOGY, SHOULDN'T WE GIVE DOCTORS THE ABILITY TO PRACTICE AS THEY SEE FIT?

For 2500 years, medical ethics has always had a bright line to keep them from doing wrong. The cardinal rule of medical ethics has been *primum non nocere* (literally, "The first thing is to do no harm"). The even older Hippocratic Oath says, "I will give no deadly medicine, even if asked." It is clear that in ancient times, as today, there were often "hard cases" in which a patient actually requested death. For good reason, doctors have resisted such pressure. Assisted suicide is *not* a new issue.

See pages
100-116

SO THERE ARE NO GRAY AREAS?

There are areas that may seem unclear at first, but if the straightforward guideline that a doctor do "no intentional killing" is followed, then clarity can be brought to an otherwise cloudy situation.

BUT HAVEN'T DOCTORS BEEN INTENTIONALLY GIVING OVERDOSES FOR A LONG TIME NOW?

When a patient is actually beginning to succumb to the ravages of cancer or some other painful illness, the doctor has always been free to aggressively deal with the pain. Many times that may mean gradually increasing the dosage over the weeks and months of treatment. In proper pain management, as the dosage spreads, the patient is kept comfortable and the controlled dosage never stupefies him or her. However, the increasing amount of opiate may have other side effects.

See pages
26-27

When the patient is *ad extremis* (that is, drawing near the point of death), there is the possibility that the amount of morphine may, as a side effect, actually suppress the breathing of the patient. The physician must carefully weigh the options. Should the patient succumb after this gradually increasing treatment, it would then be clear that the administration of the drug was for the purpose of killing the pain, not killing the patient.

This is quite a different situation than the accelerated process of using such a large dosage months earlier, when the patient has no tolerance to the drug, and the only goal being to kill the patient. In such a case, all of the familial and psychological benefits described by Dr. Kubler-Ross have been lost. Worse, the implicit trust each time a patient vulnerably presents themselves to a physician can also be lost.

When a doctor can be a killer whenever he or she thinks it is their "best medicinal judgement," then medicine will always be a potential threat to the vulnerable.

See pages 111-115

BUT IF SOMEONE HAS THE RIGHT MOTIVE, ISN'T THAT WHAT MATTERS?

The Dutch experiment proves that the genie is hard to put back in the bottle. And when it comes to motives, the darker side of human nature should also function as a warning.

See pages 64-68

Motives are very difficult to ascertain, even when an individual appears most noble. Once legalized, the temptation of an inheritance for a legacy hunter, or the "free time" that would be restored to a weary caregiver could easily tinge the decision process. Legalized physician-assisted suicide would offer an extra layer of "protection" for doctors who may feel pressed to cover up mistakes.

This possibility of hiding murder under the guise of mercy is not an idea that is only confined to prosecutors. Novelists like Agatha Christie, and socialites like Claus Von Bullow, owe their notoriety to this darker possibility.

Nurse Accuses Butler, Doctor of Killing Tobacco Heiress

By David Kocieniewski
Newsday

New York

Billionaire heiress Doris Duke was fatally drugged in a murder plot to gain her fortune, according to her nurse's sworn statement, released yesterday in Manhattan Surrogate's Court.

The butler did it, conspiring with Duke's doctor to administer a lethal injection of morphine and gain control of her $1.2 billion estate, the sworn affidavit said.

Tammy Payette, the nurse on duty during Duke's final days at her Beverly Hills mansion, said Duke was lucid and healthy before butler Bernard Lafferty said, "It's ime for Miss Duke to go" and told ⌐ Charles Kivowitz to administer ⌐doses of the pain-killer De-⌐ntember 1993.

⌐of heavy seda-

Duke knew she was mortally ill and had given a "do not resuscitate" order to doctors.

Lafferty, who will receive $5 million as co-executor of the estate, plus $500,000 a year for life, has filed a libel suit against Payette and the other Duke employees who are contesting the will. He called the accusations "frivolous yet malignant" and an attempt to cash in on Duke's riches, the larg-

Butler Bernard Lafferty called the accusations an attempt to ca⌐ the heire⌐

est e⌐
the

Lafferty has been accused of alcoholism, kidnapping two undocumented immigrants who worked at the Duke mansion, deceiving Duke and plotting her murder.

Dr. Harry Demopoulous Duke's former physician and t⌐ former executor of Duke's has charged that her med cords were tampered wⁱ change for a $500,000 b⌐

But Lafferty ch⌐ mopoulous wᵖ celve ⌐

SAN FRANCISCO CHRONICLE, January 21, 1995.

Legalizing assisted suicide will make it very tempting - and easy - to conceal an act of ill motive that previously would have been glaringly obvious.

GLOSSARY

ADVANCE DIRECTIVE - a legal document through which an individual declares his or her preference for medical treatment, in the possibility that future ability to communicate were to be impaired. Such documents include living wills and the Durable Power of Attorney for Healthcare.

ASSISTED SUICIDE - an act through which one individual facilitates the killing of another, with the latter's implied or express consent.

DEPRESSION - a serious illness which goes undiagnosed in an estimated two-thirds of cases. Depression can affect physical and emotional well-being and is a common factor in the desire for suicide.

DOUBLE EFFECT - (unintended consequences) the principle which recognizes and allows for an unintended but possible result if a desired, beneficial result is intended. This is often improperly invoked to justify intentional killing.

EUTHANASIA - the killing of an individual with ostensibly benevolent motives. Types of euthanasia include:

• voluntary euthanasia - in principle, euthanasia performed at the request of a mentally competent individual.

• non-voluntary euthanasia - euthanasia performed on an individual whose wishes are not known; e.g. the mentally incompetent, the comatose.

• involuntary euthanasia - to bring about the death of an individual against the victim's expressed wishes; compulsory euthanasia.

HEMLOCK SOCIETY - the largest and most aggressive "right-to-die" organization. Hemlock leaders have advocated euthanasia for non-terminal, debilitated individuals as well as those with terminal diagnoses.

HOSPICE - a special kind of care designed to provide treatment and support for terminally ill patients. Effective hospice is comprehensive in its approach and treats the family and patient as the "unit of care." Ethical hospice care does not include intentional killing.

MANIPULATED SUICIDE - the manuevering of persons into choosing suicide when they would not otherwise have done so. The manipulation may be oppressively coercive, or gentle and subtle. Suicidologists have suggested that such manipulation may take place even inadvertently, as a sub-conscious reaction to the needs and condition of the eventual suicide victim.

NATURAL DEATH - death that is the result of natural causes. Purposeful neglect, with the intent of causing death, does not fall under this definition.

PAIN MANAGEMENT - a comprehensive approach to treating pain, as opposed to the simple administration, or prescription of, "pain killers." Effective pain mangement requires the awareness of "total pain," the physical, emotional, and spiritual condition of the individual. It entails frequent assessment, use of various therapies, and the involvement of family and support group, as well as the wide range of pain relieving drugs.

PALLIATIVE CARE - medical treatment which is not applied for curative benefits, but to ease the discomfort and symptoms of an illness.

SEROTONIN - a neurotransmitter naturally present in the brain. Low serotonin levels have been linked to depression and suicidal behavior.

SUBSTITUTED JUDGEMENT - a legal doctrine which accepts the decisions of a surrogate as if they were the express wishes of an incapacitated individual.

RESOURCES

American Foundation for Suicide Prevention
120 Wall Street,
22nd Floor
New York, NY 10005
888-333-AFSP

Life at Risk
A Chronicle of Euthanasia Trends in America
NCCB Secretariat for Pro-life Activities
3211 4th Street NE
Washington, D.C. 20017

Medical Ethics Department
National Right to Life
419 7th Street NW
Suite 400
Washington, D.C. 20004

Publishes *Will to Live*, a protective power of attorney for healthcare, as well as numerous papers on bioethics .

National Legal Center
for the Medically Dependent and Disabled
Box 1586
Terre Haute, IN 47808-1586

Functions as legal advocates for the vulnerable. Publishes *Issues in Law and Medicine*, a scholarly review dedicated to the public policy aspects of bioethics.

INDEX

DID YOU BORROW THIS BOOK?

If you would like to own your own copy *of DEATH AS A SALESMAN: What's Wrong With Assisted Suicide,* or if you know of a friend or loved one who could benefit from a fresh perspective on this issue, please copy the coupon below.

If you wish you may order directly on the New Regency Publishing order line - 1(800) BOOK; NEW   (800) 266-5639

Quantity Discounts available.

Send to : New Regency Publishing, Publisher's Circle Box 1443, Sacramento, CA 95812 **www.nrpub.com**